hey marketers,
get your priorities straight

#marketingpriorities

Join the conversation about setting marketing priorities by using #marketingpriorities on your preferred social networks. Share the marketing tactics you've prioritized and those you've decided to skip.

LITTLE SHOE PUBLISHING
Hey Marketers, Get Your Priorities Straight
Nicholas Scarpino

Cover and Interior Design: Nicholas Scarpino
Foreword: Avinash Kaushik

This book was self-published by the author, Nicholas Scarpino, under Little Shoe Publishing

The ideas and opinions expressed in this book are those of the author only, and do not represent those of any company or organization

Published in the United States
ISBN 978-0-9891334-0-1

Version 1.0
Printed by CreateSpace, a DBA of On-Demand Publishing, LLC

For my wife and children,
my top priorities

about the author
Nick Scarpino

Nick Scarpino works at Google, where he uses data to uncover consumer insights for marketers. In his spare time, he writes a popular marketing blog called *Never a Lack of Ideas*. Over the last 10+ years, Nick has had the opportunity to work in marketing at startups, small businesses, and non-profit organizations. Nick's marketing work has earned numerous national awards for excellence.

Nick has a Bachelor's Degree in Marketing from the University of Notre Dame and a Master's Degree in Integrated Marketing Communications from Northwestern University.

Nick is passionate about helping companies of all sizes develop engaging marketing communication programs. This is the first book Nick has written and he did so by burning the midnight oil for several months in a row. Nick is also the creator, designer, and publisher of the family card game, *What's Wild?!*.

contents
prepare yourself

foreword
by Avinash Kaushik

If there is one incredible blessing in the marketing world today, it is choice. As business owners, we can do anything we set our mind to. Things that were previously only accessible to massive companies with *massiver* budgets are available to any mom-and-pop business. How awesome!

If there is one incredible curse in the marketing world today, it is choice. Limitless possibilities offer nothing short of instantaneous paralysis.

For you, the latter should not be a problem. You've got this book!

In eight chapters over a short 107 pages, Nick will hold your hand and help you navigate the complexity of marketing as it exists today, help you create a plan that will use your (surely limited) budget wisely, and get the highest possible return.

An example of the value you'll get is illustrated in the 2x2 framework in Chapter Five. I promise, you are going to have this printed out, scrawled over, and posted on your office wall — as you ensure that your marketing is targeted optimally while delivering on the promise to amplify your brand value via sharing.

Another example is Chapter Six, The Five Must-Haves. Nick takes the entire space we play in and boils it down to five simple tactics that you must have. The end result is efficient engagement between customers and your brand, and scalable communication, online or offline.

Good marketing provides access to amazing possibilities. Use this book to crush your competition and create engaged audiences.

I wish you all the best!

– Avinash Kaushik
 Author of *Web Analytics 2.0* and *Web Analytics: An Hour A Day*

preface
about this book

There are nearly six million businesses in the United States with fewer than 100 employees[1]. Most of these companies have fewer than five people working exclusively in marketing roles. In fact, many of these companies don't even have a single person dedicated exclusively to marketing. This book is meant for these types of companies. This book is for the team of three bakers looking to open their second shop within the next two years. It's for the dentist of 20 years down the street looking to build his business. It's for the lawyer who has started her own practice but doesn't know how to attract new customers. It's for the church or other non-profit organization looking to build its member base and increase donations. And yes, it's even for the technology startup that knows it has to bring in customers while still perfecting its platform.

I love companies of this size because they can make decisions quickly and implement great ideas. They can build great brands based on real, meaningful relationships with customers. They're scrappy, creative, and know how to hustle to get things done. But many of them have so many things other than marketing on which they need to focus — like securing funding, focusing on building great products and services, expanding distribution, and on and on. By the time a small

---

[1]According to the US Census

business is ready to think about building a website, creating a sales kit, or sponsoring an event, it doesn't have time or money to invest in something that won't help grow the business. Small businesses need marketing communications that both build their brand and directly impact the bottom line.

What do I mean by "marketing communications?" Well, there are many aspects of marketing; namely, the traditionally accepted "Four Ps:" product features, pricing, placement (otherwise known as "distribution"), and promotion. Volumes of books have been written on each of these Four Ps. This book focuses exclusively on the last one — promoting your product or service — and I call it by its all-encompassing name: marketing communication.

If I had it my way, marketing scholars would add another "p" to their four, and of course, it would be "prioritization." I think it's that important, especially for startups, small businesses, and non-profit organizations.

It's easy for marketers in small businesses to quickly feel like they are drowning in a sea of to-do lists. And while there are never concrete answers in marketing — after all, nobody can tell the future — there are principles for making marketing communications decisions that have been tested through time. This book provides guidance for making these decisions and taking the guesswork out of setting marketing communication priorities, given our world of imperfect information.

In this book, I walk through an easy-to-understand visual framework by which all marketing communication tactics should be considered; so as new marketing options come and go, you'll know which ones to embrace and which ones to forget. I also outline the five must-have things all marketers must do before anything else. Real-life examples are everywhere in this book, making it easy to see exactly how the entire process works. By the end of this book, you will be able to:

- Start a marketing communications program (if you haven't already) by beginning with the five marketing communication tactics you must do before anything else.

- Prioritize the current marketing ideas in your head and identify which ones to do first and which ones to skip.

- Prioritize future marketing communication ideas as they arise. When the next big social media website presents an advertising opportunity, you'll know whether or not it will be worth the effort.

I intentionally kept this book to a reasonable length. (That means it's fairly short and easily digestible.) Why? Because it's hyper-focused on helping you set priorities. I've prioritized the topic of setting priorities and remained focused on that single topic throughout the book.

This book is not a set of recommended marketing tactics. Rather, it's a framework for prioritizing the initiatives you are likely already considering. I'm not going to tell you that you'll be wildly successful if you maintain a great social media account. Or that the trade show at the end of the year is going to produce the most sales leads for you. Marketing platforms come and go quickly these days. This book outlines ways in which to prioritize marketing communications today, and will help guide your way when everything changes in a few years, as will surely happen.

This is not a book for companies with marketing departments of 20 people. Nor is it a book for companies who have small marketing departments but outsource most of their work to agencies. Marketing functions within these types of companies are much different than their small business counterparts. Companies with large marketing departments or a lot of agency support have much higher budgets and have the luxury of testing a wide variety of custom marketing tactics to see which ones work best.

Many startups, small businesses, and non-profit organizations might consider marketing as an expense they can't afford to spare. They may not see it as an investment that can help grow a business or charitable cause. (Perhaps you are nodding your head in agreement right now.) While these organizations may be willing to test the waters with a few marketing tactics, they don't have the margin of error that their larger counterparts have. When you're a small but mighty team of marketers or even just a single person who has to wear the marketing hat for the company, prioritization matters. There's no room for error.

There's also a difference in specialization between small and large marketing teams. Marketers within small businesses have to execute with excellence across a wide variety of marketing tactics. Marketers within large companies are able to become specialists on just a few tactics and therefore require a different level of marketing knowledge.

This book is mostly for business to consumer marketers and non-profit organizations, although you'll probably find value in the lessons contained here if you market only to other businesses, as well. You should know, though, that all of the examples discussed reference business to consumer and non-profit marketing.

What This Book Is Not

This is not a book on how to create high-level marketing strategy. There are plenty of books on that topic. Allow me to give you an example of the difference between a strategy and a tactic:

If your goal is to create a successful pizza restaurant, you might have a few different marketing strategies for doing so:

- Creating a family-friendly environment
- Staying open late on weekends
- Having ultra-fast delivery to the nearby area

Those strategies are also your value propositions. I'm not here to help you determine your value propositions. I'm here to help you prioritize marketing communication tactics to promote these strategies. Examples of marketing communication tactics to promote these strategies are:

- Hiring a man in a gorilla costume to distribute fliers in front of the restaurant
- Placing a coupon in the local newspaper
- Advertising on the Internet against local searches for pizzerias
- Starting a Twitter account
- Sponsoring a pizza night at a local school's Parent Teacher Association meeting

This book assumes you've identified a consumer need based on a set of insights, and you've created a compelling product or service to fulfill that need. I assume you've identified your value proposition and are struggling to identify the right ways to tell people about that proposition.

Why This Author?

Over the last 10+ years, I have had the unique opportunity to work in marketing at a startup I created, a non-profit organization, and a small business. I have been fortunate to work in marketing at the smallest companies (just me) and one of the largest in the world (Google). I know how tough it can be to prioritize marketing communication initiatives within small businesses. And I've actually executed countless marketing communication campaigns with success, so I know how to take something from an idea to the real world.

Now, I haven't been successful in everything I've done professionally; I've definitely made many mistakes. But, I've learned a lot along the way and I've been developing the thoughts and frameworks in this book over the last ten years. So, you're in good hands. If you care to agree or disagree with my ideas in this book, don't hesitate to look me up at **www.nickscarpino.com** and let me know your thoughts.

hey marketers, get your priorities straight

setting marketing communication priorities at startups, small businesses, and non-profits

NICK SCARPINO

chapter 1
the need for priorities

A few years ago, I was organizing the production of a new photo directory for my church. The printed directory would eventually include photos and contact information for a few hundred families and would be mailed to their homes. The project required more work than I could take on myself, so I decided to work with a small photography business to get the job done. After meeting with a sales representative from the photography company to go over the details, the gentleman left me with a folder with information about additional products and services we could consider buying in the future. When I got home that night and opened it up, I was shocked at what I saw — there were 34 fliers and brochures advertising different products and services inside the folder.

34!

Yes, I counted every single one of them and I even took the photo you see on the next page. Now, I'm sure there was great information on those fliers, but how was I supposed to sift through it all? I didn't have that kind of time. And where was I supposed to start? I was intimidated and overwhelmed. I was hoping for some guidance after our meeting, but I was left with information overload.

Maybe 34 fliers was just a few too many for one sales kit.

I was recently online buying some gift cards from a locally-owned restaurant. While on the restaurant's website, I saw something that has become pretty standard on websites these days: a row of icons along the top linked to several social media sites like Facebook, Twitter, Google+, Pinterest, etc. You've seen this before. But when I clicked on the Twitter logo, I saw a Twitter profile with only a handful of followers and just two posts — the last post had been made months prior. Sure enough, when I clicked on the Facebook link, I was also greeted with a page that hadn't been updated in months.

How does something like this happen?

Well, the 34 fliers are not the problem. And neither are the social media sites void of content. They are just symptoms of an overall problem; not setting marketing communication priorities. The fliers are indicative of a company trying to promote every single thing it is doing. The empty social media sites show a company trying to chase every new marketing communication option available, but not having the time to do any of them well.

You see, there are an infinite number of great marketing ideas in this world. And it's very easy to try to act on all of them — especially in a startup, small business, or a non-profit organization, where marketers can be quick to act. But without some direction, it can be impossible to identify which marketing ideas will build powerful brands and lead to the best returns on investment. As the ideas pile up, so do the to-do lists. A company's marketing communication efforts can die a slow death under the pile of these to-do lists.

I call it "death by to-do lists." And it's a very real problem marketers face every day.

Noted psychologist Barry Schwartz studies what happens to people when faced with complete freedom of choice. In his 2004 book, *The Paradox of Choice,* he writes that an abundance of choice can be paralyzing and exhausting to the human psyche. A seemingly endless list of choices can actually prevent people from making a decision. In order for us to make a decision and feel good about it, he writes, we need to narrow our list of choices to a few that meet certain criteria, and then decide from there. And that's the point of this book — to provide a framework for helping marketers prioritize the marketing opportunities that provide the best chance for success.

Regrettably, I've been contributing to the confusion about setting marketing priorities. In 2009, I started to write about engaging marketing ideas on my blog, *Never a Lack of Ideas.* My goal at the time was to gather great ideas in one place and inspire marketers in new ways. But I realize that by ending every post with the message, "add this to your to-do list," I've only been piling the ideas on top of marketers and I've done nothing to help provide ideas on making marketing priorities.

Yikes. I've spent years contributing to this problem. But at least I'm not the only one.

Search Amazon for books on marketing and you'll find nearly a half million results. That's a lot of noise and a lot of ideas. You'll find thousands of books on creating winning marketing strategies, but you won't find any on prioritizing marketing tactics to execute that strategy. It's sexy to talk about strategy, but getting down to identifying the appropriate marketing tactics gets a whole lot messier.

So what's a small business marketer to do? How does marketing fit in if you've already come up with a great business strategy? How should you spend your limited time and money in order to maximize return on marketing spend? Should you invest in billboard advertisements or spend time building a presence on Twitter? Should you invest in a customer call center or spend money on distributing coupons through the Sunday newspaper? By the end of this book, you'll know the answers to these questions because I provide a framework for making these types of decisions.

Let's Begin

In the next four chapters, we'll walk through the three most important factors in setting marketing communication priorities. After describing each factor in detail, we'll look at a way to combine all three into a graph on which you'll plot all of the marketing communication tactics you're considering. Then, you'll be able to see which ones you should prioritize and which ones you should put on the back burner.

Next, we'll discuss the five must-have tactics on which all successful marketing communications programs are built. To bring everything together, I've included a case study of the best example of setting marketing priorities that I've ever seen — and it's one you've likely never heard of.

chapter 2
focus on the target market

Two years after I graduated from college, I was interviewing for a marketing position at a small non-profit organization in a suburb of Chicago. The marketing department at the company consisted of three people: a Director of Marketing, a part-time Marketing Coordinator, and a full-time Marketing Manager who had just left the company. I was interviewing for the Manager position. In my interview with the Director, he gave me a little marketing quiz. He asked me:

For every marketing promotion we do, there are always three important things to consider. Which of these three is the most important?

- *The offer*
- *The target market*
- *The look and feel of the message*

I sat in my chair and squirmed just a little — the question made me uneasy because I hadn't really thought about marketing promotions in this way before. I actually asked the Director to give me a minute to think about it, and I wrote my three options on a piece of paper. Finally, I looked up at him and said, "the target market is always the most important."

"Very good," he said. Later that week, he offered me the job. I respectfully declined the offer, but that's not the point of this story. The point of this story is that in marketing, the target market is always the most important consideration. It's the very first consideration marketers should make before taking any marketing action.

Putting this rule into practice, though, is the hard part. First, you have to recognize that you may have multiple target markets. At a fundamental level, you may have a target market of existing customers — those who have purchased your products before — and a target market of potential customers who have not purchased from you before. That's pretty obvious, but your marketing messages to each group may be completely different. At a more detailed level, you can, and should, segment (that's the fancy way marketers say "divide") these two groups with more granularity. It is very important to:

- Drill down into the characteristics of customers,
- Segment them into different groups of customers based on those characteristics, and
- Prioritize which groups of customers you want to target.

Once you have prioritized your different markets, you are perfectly equipped to figure out how much time and money you would pay to reach each one. The higher priority markets warrant spending more time and money to reach.

Identifying Target Markets When You Haven't Had Any Customers

There are plenty of great customer segmentation frameworks for identifying priority markets if you know a little bit of information about your existing customers. We'll discuss two of those frameworks in a little bit. But if you're trying to target customers who have never purchased from you before, it can be a little tricky. How old will your best customers be? Where will they live? Why will they buy your products or donate to your cause? And how will you even begin to answer these questions?

To start with, I've seen first-hand at Google that the very best potential customer you can have is one who is actively searching for something you sell or the type of cause you support. People searching for your product or service always comprise your most important target market.

In graduate school at Northwestern University, I had a professor named Randy Hlavac who is a brilliant direct marketer. He teaches students about two groups of target markets: passion markets (or "pay-shun" markets, as he called them) and trigger markets. I still can't figure out why he said "passion" the way he did — he is originally from Nebraska — but it was certainly memorable. I love his way of thinking about target markets because it doesn't require any existing customer data; so the customer groups can be applied immediately by startups, non-profits, and small businesses.

So, the best way to identify priority target markets if you've never had any customers is to think of customers in terms of their:

- Search behaviors
- Passions
- Triggers

Let's discuss each of the three groups.

Searchers

Do you know where the term "marketing" comes from? One theory states that a long time ago, merchants used to sell nearly all their wares in a town's marketplace. They would gather up their products, push their carts to the common marketplace, set up shop, and try to sell as much as possible. Different merchants took different approaches to their marketplace strategies: some would yell and shout at customers walking by; others relied on the quality of their workmanship or freshness of their food to sell their goods. But the vast majority of the town's commerce took place at that central marketplace. Everyone knew to go there if they wanted to buy something.

The important point here is that a long time ago, merchants realized that the best way to sell things is to establish a place in which buyers could come and look for things to buy. Why? Because the best potential customer was someone actually looking to buy something.

Fast forward a few thousand years. Customers are still looking for things to buy, but they're looking in stores (like the *supermarket*) and on the Internet now. They're searching for entertainment via their XBox consoles, over Wi-Fi connections on airplanes, and at kiosks in the mall. They're searching for children's toys on Craig's List, Ebay, and Amazon. So, while the number of locations in which customers can look for products has increased exponentially since the days of the common marketplace, the principle is still very much the same. *The very best potential customer you have is one who is actively looking to buy something that you sell.*

So how does this fit into your efforts to set marketing communication priorities? It's really quite simple: if you aren't prioritizing marketing tactics that reach the people who are actively searching for the products you sell or the causes you support, you're leaving money on the table. These are your best potential customers. If you own a brick-and-mortar store, it's essential that you prioritize communication programs that engage customers regardless of whether they buy something from you. After all, they actually took time out of their busy lives to walk into your store. Of course, you'd like everyone who walks in to buy something, but if they don't, you must equip them to remember to come back or to tell someone else about your store. (Don't worry; we'll cover this in great detail in the next chapter.)

Next, think about where people go to find the things they are looking to buy. Maybe they ask their friends. Maybe they look in the phone book. Most of them probably go online. Ask your friends and family what they do.

Regardless of whether or not your business exists only on the Internet, you must reach the people looking for your products and services online. If you do a search on a search engine or on Amazon for your best-selling product, does your product or website appear in the results? If not, then you're missing a golden opportunity. Not appearing in the results for relevant search queries is equivalent to not even pushing your cart to the ancient marketplace and setting up shop. You're not even in that potential customer's consideration set. That's not good. Ensuring that potential customers and donors are able to find your offerings online must be one of your top marketing priorities.

If you're not sure how to begin finding your searchers online, I've included some specific recommendations in Chapter Six.

Passion Markets

The idea behind passion markets is simple: when thinking about customers who will eventually consume your products or services or donate to your causes, think about groups of people that are passionate about something with which your product aligns. These groups are the people who have been directly affected by the rare disease your organization is trying to eliminate. Or they love collecting antique clocks and would love to have you restore them as part of your new business. These types of people spend their discretionary income on their passions, hobbies, and collections. These will be the people who tell their friends about your business and will be your most loyal customers or supporters.

We find these super-users at the intersection of passionate groups of people and a brand that provides ways to enhance the experiences of these groups. These groups of people have the potential to be your best customers and they'll tell all their friends about you. Think of the people who wear head-to-toe Harley Davidson gear or the teenagers who will pay your company money to wear your logo on t-shirts.

To illustrate this point, let's look at an example of a passion market: people who love to garden. There are many products and services that align with gardening. The most obvious ones are gardening tools and supplies, seeds, outdoor gardening clothing, and books about gardening. But if we take a step back and consider why people like gardening, we can see how other products and services can be aligned with this passion market:

- Some gardeners grow their own fruits and vegetables because they like sustainable, organic foods. Perhaps they may be interested in organic cookbooks and sustainabilty products like composters and compostable dishware.

- Some gardeners grow flowers because they love their beauty. They may also be interested in bringing that beauty into their home with unique flowerpots and vases.

- Some people garden because they love the outdoors. Perhaps they may be interested in other outdoor activities like camping at a nearby campground on the weekend or hiking in the closest state park.

If you can identify groups of people that are already passionate about something for which your product, service, or cause aligns, you will have a captive audience to target with your marketing communications.

Trigger Markets

Trigger markets are created when people go through big changes in their lives and are therefore "triggered" into being in your target market. If you can identify the triggers that make your products, services, or causes suddenly relevant to a group of people, you'll identify a great target market for your products.

For example, if you are an independent financial planner, one of your target markets should be nearby new parents. New parents are the types of people who suddenly find themselves in the market for life insurance, disability insurance, and other long-term financial products. Since going through one of the biggest changes of their lives, they've been triggered into thinking much differently about their finances and taking care of their family than they have been in the past.

Other trigger markets for independent financial planners would be new college graduates who may be interested in retirement planning at a young age, early retirees looking to stretch their retirement dollars as far as possible, and new widows or widowers trying to manage their money without the help of their partner. Identifying ways to target these groups of trigger markets is key to an independent financial planner's successful marketing communication program.

As another example, let's say you are the only person working in marketing at a non-profit botanic garden. Think through the life events that may trigger people into considering going to your garden. You will immediately think of: people looking to hold their weddings in your beautiful setting, high school and college graduates looking to take their senior class pictures, and people looking to hold retirement parties in a great location. Thinking back to passion markets, the garden would identify botany enthusiasts and photographers as easy passion markets to target. By identifying these trigger and passion markets, you can begin to find marketing communication solutions that target these specific markets.

Identifying Target Markets When You Already Have Customers — The RFM Model

Prioritizing target markets is a bit easier if you have already had some customers. If you've recorded some data about them, you can use that data to segment your customers into similar groups. Once you've put them into groups, you can create marketing communications for each group.

If you have had customers but haven't recorded any data about them, you need to start doing so. Looking at customer data will likely open your eyes to customer segments and target markets you never knew you had. See Chapter Six for suggestions on how to start a customer database and read the rest of this chapter as a guide for what types of data to collect in order to best segment your customers.

There are many models you can use for customer segmentation, but I think the best one to start with is called the RFM model, or "Recency, Frequency, and Monetary" model. (I didn't invent this model, I'm just a fan and advocate.) While this model assumes customers will behave in the future as they have in the past, we all know that's not necessarily the case, so be aware of that before you start using it. Despite this shortcoming, as a framework for thinking about ways to prioritize target markets, this model is a wonderful place to start.

Recency

"Recency" states there is a high correlation between the date of the most recent purchase a customer has made and the date of her next purchase. Therefore, recency can be used to predict your best future customers. It could be that your best future customer is the one who purchased from you yesterday. And for many marketers, this is the case. That's why we often receive a coupon by email right after making an online purchase, or we get one inside the box of an item that we received in the mail. In this case, customers who purchased most recently should be given high priority with your marketing initiatives.

But for other businesses, the best future customer might not be the most recent customer. In seasonal businesses, for example, the best potential customer may be one who ordered exactly a year ago. Or perhaps the best customer is one whose birthday is today. In these cases, customers who ordered at specific rolling dates should be given high priority with your marketing initiatives.

Frequency

"Frequency" states there is a high correlation between the frequency a customer purchases and the likelihood that she will purchase in the future. Therefore, frequency can be used to predict your best future customers. If you own a small coffee shop, you place a high value on your regular customers — those who come in five times per week. Or, perhaps you work at a church or non-profit group that receives 80% of its revenue from customers who donate regularly on a weekly or monthly basis.

In both of these scenarios, these customers are your "regulars" and are your best potential future customers, barring any big life changes like moving, losing a job, etc. That's why we encourage our regulars to sign up for email newsletters and become fans of ours on Facebook. We can build relationships with them and give them customized incentives to continue being our best customers. In this case, customers who frequent your business or donate to your cause most frequently should be given high priority with your marketing initiatives.

Monetary

"Monetary" states there is a high correlation between the amount of money a customer has spent with you in the past and the likelihood that she will purchase in the future. It could be that the more money a customer has spent with you, the greater chance that person will be one of your best future customers. My favorite example of this comes from a personal story. I like to shop at Banana Republic, and there is an outlet store fairly close to my house. I haven't been to the store recently (recency), and I don't go there very often (frequency). However, I know that the next time I go I'm going to stock up on clothing and spend a lot of money. To Banana Republic, I'm a great example of a high-value customer because of my monetary value.

Using only recency and frequency measures to prioritize customers would leave out the people, for example, who may drive a long way to spend crazy amounts of money at your business every so often. Regardless of their reasons, customers who have spent large amounts of money with your business in the past should be given high priority with your marketing initiatives.

Putting RFM Together

Once you have in place ways to measure the recency, frequency, and monetary value of your customers or donors, you need to use the data to form groups of customers that have similar RFM profiles. Sophisticated marketers will use statistical software packages to group customers into segments, but you may not have the time or skill set to do this type of work. I highly encourage you to strive for this level of precise analysis over time, but for now, we'll just use averages to group our customers.

Let's look at an example of how you might create a basic spreadsheet of customer data to inform how you will create different customer segments.

Customer name	Days since most recent purchase	# of purchases	Average purchase size	Customer value (Column 3 x 4)
Steady Eddy	7	50	$50	$2,500
Yearly Yolanda	150	2	$1,000	$2,000
Long Lost Larry	438	10	$100	$1,000

In the example above, we see purchase histories for three different customers. As you may have already noticed, the second, third, and fourth columns reflect recency, frequency, and monetary value. The final column identifies a total value of the customer, based on multiplying the number of purchases by the average purchase size.

Let's interpret what we see about these three customers:

- **Steady Eddy's** most recent purchase was just seven days ago. Perhaps that indicates he is a frequent customer, but not necessarily. He has purchased from us 50 times and out of a sample of three customers, that's a lot. His average purchase size is smallest of the three at only $50, but out of our three customers, he's the most valuable.

- **Yearly Yolanda** last made a purchase about five months ago. Perhaps she only buys on a yearly basis, but not necessarily. She has only made two purchases in the past, but they have averaged $1,000 per purchase, which is a lot of money. That makes her the second most valuable customer here.

- **Long Lost Larry** hasn't bought from us in more than a year. He has made 10 purchases from us in the past, and they were fairly valuable at $100 each. He's valuable as a customer, but not as much as the first two customers.

As you can see, RFM measures give us a baseline for understanding these three customers. We don't know anything about why they've purchased in the past, but we know how valuable they have been to our business. Our ultimate goal as marketers is to increase the values in the final column — each customer's overall value. Since the first step is understanding that overall value, we're off to a good start with just these three simple measures.

So what do we do with this information? Let's go one step further now and add another column called "marketing goal." Let's identify one opportunity for each of these three customers:

Customer name	Days since most recent purchase	# of purchases	Average purchase size	Customer value (Column 3 x 4)	Marketing Goal
Steady Eddy	7	50	$50	$2,500	Increase average purchase size
Yearly Yolanda	150	2	$1,000	$2,000	Increase purchase frequency
Long Lost Larry	438	10	$100	$1,000	Come back and try us again

As you can see, our goal for Steady Eddy is to increase his average purchase size. He's clearly a regular customer. We just want to use marketing communication tactics to incentivize him to spend more with us.

Our goal for Yearly Yolanda is for her to increase her purchase frequency. If we can increase her purchases to two or more per year, it's likely that she will become much more valuable. If we can figure out what may incentivize her to purchase more frequently and then communicate that to her, we will increase her overall value to us.

Long Lost Larry hasn't purchased from us in a long time. But when he used to purchase, he was a good customer. Our goal for Larry is to get him to come back and try us again. Our marketing communications should incentivize him to do so.

Our "Marketing Goal" column is really our first attempt at answering the question of *what* to tell each group of customers. The only drawback, of course, is that it only takes into consideration what *we* want to tell our customers, and not what they want to hear from us. In Chapter Three, we'll discuss the importance of communicating in a way that gives customers meaningful, remarkable experiences. Until then, let's get back to our customer segmentation example.

Moving from Customers to Customer Segments

We just walked through a very basic example showing just three customers. The concepts used in that example are the same as those for creating customer segments — groups of customers with similar characteristics. But instead of using single numbers for recency, frequency, and monetary values, we group sets of customers by ranges of RFM. Let's look at an example:

Customer segment	Days since most recent purchase	# of purchases	Average purchase size
Small-Cart Steady Eddies	1-15	30+	<$200
Yearly Purchasers	100-182	1-10	$500
Lost Good Customers	365+	5+	$100+

Now we've provided a framework by which we can group our existing customers. Customers whose RFM profiles fall into these ranges are lumped into these segments. Then, we can design marketing communications for each group. Of course, there are an infinite number of ways to group customers and continually testing different segmentation methods is part of the fun of marketing.

Prioritizing These Segments

Now that we've grouped our customers into segments, we need to prioritize them. At this point, the best way to prioritize which markets to target with our first efforts and dollars is to target the market that brings in the most revenue. In two chapters, we'll talk about return on marketing investment, which takes into consideration the cost of reaching customers. But as you're just getting started in establishing priorities, you should pick the group of existing customers that brings in the most revenue per customer.

That last part is important: "per customer." There's a good chance that your organization follows the 80/20 rule of customers: that is, 80% of your revenue comes from only 20% of your customers or donors. If you lumped all of your customers into segments based on RFM, there's a decent chance you would see a lot of customers (the 80% who don't purchase or donate much) end up in one or two large segments.

If you were to prioritize your marketing communications based on the number of customers in each of the segments, you would likely make the mistake of focusing on a large group of customers that may be difficult to reach or tough to convince to buy or donate more. Instead, prioritize the segments that bring in the most money per customer.

Going Beyond Recency, Frequency, and Monetary Value

Recency, frequency, and monetary value are just guidelines for starting to identify metrics that will enable you to target your highest priority markets. But you can, and should, add your own factors, as well. I call enhancements to the RFM model the "RFM+ model." (Catchy, isn't it?) There are scores of other customer metrics you can look at, but I suggest that you look at least two more: zip code and birthdate.

Zip Code

A person's zip code reveals a lot. Many websites will show demographic information about the population in each zip code, but in my opinion, the best ones are from Nielsen and Esri. If you do a web search for "Nielsen PRIZM zip code" or "Esri zip code lookup," you'll find them right away. These sites will show you the typical household income range of people who live in a particular zip code. They will also show you the type of people who typically live in the zip code, whether it be double-income earners without kids; low income, mostly-single residents; and everything in between. Best of all, these tools are completely free.

At a basic level, zip codes also tell you the time zone in which people live, which gives insight into their media consumption patterns. For example, someone living on the east coast might be surfing on a tablet at home at 8:00 pm, but at the same moment in time in the west coast, an office worker is likely getting off work and commuting home, possibly listening to the radio or looking at a smartphone.

If you have a product in a store or actually own a store, creating target markets based on zip codes is key to prioritizing your marketing communications. Obviously, you would want to prioritize the zip codes closest to your store or where your products are available.

Birth Date

Like zip code, a person's birth date also reveals a lot. Most obviously, it tells you someone's age. If you sell a product or service targeted at a specific age range, birth date will help you narrow your target market quickly. Knowing someone's birthday also provides the perfect opportunity to market to a trigger market based on a milestone birthday. Often times, when a person turns 30, 40, 50, or 60, she wants to celebrate in a larger than normal way. The 16th and 21st birthdays also carry significant value in someone's life and call for different kinds of celebrations and gifts. If you can identify appropriate triggers for your product or service based on someone's age, you can create target markets of similar people, based simply on their birth date.

Other Demographics

In addition to birth date, there are many other demographic factors that may be relevant to identifying your most lucrative target markets. Some demographic characteristics are easier to gather than others, and the value of these characteristics vary depending on your business.

For example, sex may be a key factor in segmenting your customers. If you sell custom-made women's headbands through your own website and a shop on Etsy, your consumers will most likely be female. However, you may have a customer base of men looking to buy gifts for their daughters, wives, girlfriends, mothers, nieces, etc. Your marketing messages to each sex should be completely different.

Continuing this example, there are at least two easy ways to help figure out whether or not a customer is male or female:

1. **Just ask.** It's easy to just ask your customers their sex in your online registration and order forms. If you'd like, you can make that field optional on the form so customers don't feel like they're giving too much personal information. (Note that simply asking is often the easiest way to find out anything about any of your customers.)

2. **Allow customers to identify when a product is a gift.** Again, if you sell products or services online, consider asking customers to check a box if their purchase is a gift. If you sell products mostly geared toward women, for example, checking this box

at least identifies a customer who may be a man. He or she may not be a man, but it at least opens up the possibility. Every little piece of information like this goes a long way in building consumer profiles and target market segments.

The list of other demographic data you may wish to collect from customers is quite long. Some demographic data can be much more difficult to collect from customers. In fact, some customers don't want to share with companies more information about themselves than is absolutely necessary, so always keep that in mind when deciding what information you absolutely need compared to what is nice to know but optional. To get you thinking about additional factors for your target markets, consider:

- Household income
- Marital status
- Number of children in the household
- Occupation
- Smartphone owners
- Home ownership vs. renting
- Ethnicity
- Religion

Drawbacks to the RFM and RFM+ Models

There are many cases in which a company's best future customer is not one who has ever purchased from it before, and, therefore, the RFM and RFM+ models won't work. Sometimes these situations involve very expensive one-time purchases. For example, a man who is shopping for an engagement ring for his girlfriend may be the best future customer for a jewelry store. If he's never purchased jewelry from the store before, there's no good way to use his previous purchases to predict his future purchase. In order to target groups of people who have never been customers before, I recommend looking at searchers, passion markets, and trigger markets, like we discussed in the beginning of this chapter.

Summary

There are many different ways to identify your most important target markets. Whether you're looking at searchers, passion markets, trigger markets, an RFM model, or an RFM+ model, the important thing to remember is to always prioritize marketing communication tactics that reach your target markets. Measure as much as you can about your customers so you can test different hypotheses about your target markets and make adjustments as you evolve. If you've never had a customer, it's important to install processes to measure RFM and other metrics as soon as possible. Then when you acquire customers, you can immediately begin testing to see if your target market hypotheses were correct.

Ultimately, your goal as a marketer is to maximize the lifetime value of each customer within a target market. We will cover this much more in Chapter Four, but it's worth mentioning at this point so we don't lose sight of our overall goal when building target market models. As you build advanced RFM and RFM+ models, you will identify the groups of customers that are worth the most money over time.

chapter 3
create shareable experiences

Imagine you have just spent five hours flying on an airplane late at night on Christmas Eve to visit your family. You just exited the plane. You are exhausted and anxious to collect your bags so you can see your family as quickly as possible. As the baggage claim conveyor belt starts, you notice something strange — instead of your bags coming out, you see beautiful, hand-wrapped gifts. As you and your fellow passengers wonder what's going on, you notice that one of the gifts has your name on it. You're skeptical at first, but then you open it to find a cute teddy bear with a Santa hat, compliments of the airline.

You're suddenly re-energized after your long flight and thankful for the little surprise. You and your fellow passengers begin taking pictures and videos of the spectacle, and start emailing your friends, posting the photos to Facebook and the videos to YouTube. Shortly afterward, you are able to collect your bag and leave the airport to visit your family. What's the first thing you tell them about when you arrive? Of course, you tell them all about the fun little gift that you just received from the airline.

European airline SpanAir was responsible for bringing this idea to life. The airline surprised and delighted 190 passengers in this way on Christmas Eve in 2010. Why? Because the company knew that the most powerful form of marketing is a recommendation from a friend. With these presents, SpanAir made 190 people happy and found a way to get those people to tell all of their friends and family about how great SpanAir is. They videoed the gift-giving event and then posted videos to YouTube in both English and Spanish. Those videos received more than a million views, combined. The airline targeted just 190 passengers but reached more than a million people with its message.

That's the power of word-of-mouth marketing. In fact, in nearly every single product category, you'll find research showing the best, most popular sales referral source is a personal referral. I won't bore you with paragraphs of facts and figures from the research. Hopefully you'll take my word for it — word-of-mouth marketing matters.

Now, the ultimate goal for every marketer is to convince consumers to buy more products or services. That's the revenue side of the equation. Said another way, marketing programs must be measured on their ability to bring in money. Of course, it's equally important for marketers to find ways to do this as inexpensively as possible. When we combine a need for increased revenue with the need for keeping costs low, we can calculate a return on marketing investment. The goal is to have the highest return on marketing investment with the dollars we're allowed to invest (and then, of course, fight for more dollars, based on our success).

The absolute cheapest way for a company to grow quickly is to provide such an amazing product or service that consumers tell their friends and family about it. Customers become evangelists for your brand, which costs you nothing. The same can be said about great marketing. In everything that you do as a marketer, you need to ask yourself, "Would someone tell a friend about this?" And, "Did I enable someone to tell their friends about this?" Did you provide such great customer service over the phone that someone would brag to her friends about it? Is your website so quick and easy to use that the next time my sister is looking to buy something similar I would recommend she visit your site? Did you include a little "If you liked this product, rate us online," card when you shipped your package?

I've just touched on the two aspects of creating shareable experiences, which is the second factor to look at in order to prioritize marketing communications. There are two aspects to creating shareable experiences: the first is creating content and experiences that are so compelling someone will want to tell a friend about them. The second is enabling the target market to share about the compelling experience you gave them. These two aspects are best revealed by answering two simple questions:

1. Have you given customers an experience worth sharing?
2. Have you helped them share about it?

Let's dive deeper into each of these two components.

Creating Compelling Experiences

Plain, old, traditional advertising in which an advertiser shouts to anybody within earshot about their great offer is really boring. Not many people see a car advertisement on television and then go tell their friends about it. (Outside of Super Bowl ads, that is.) Why? Because the content of the advertisement isn't memorable. It's not remarkable.

When marketing communications are not remarkable, they are not spread organically. That means advertisers have to pay for every single pair of eyes and ears that consume the message. While that's fine for large brands with enormous marketing budgets, that won't fly for startups, small businesses, and non-profit organizations. As a small business, you need your message to spread like wildfire for free.

The only way to do that is to create experiences with your marketing communications that are worth sharing.

Creating amazing experiences with your marketing communications is not just about creating the next big YouTube "viral video." In fact, if that's your goal, you're not approaching it right. It's about understanding your target markets and creating content that they actually want to consume. This content needs to add value to their already busy lives. In fact, it needs to add so much value that your target market can't wait to tell their friends about it, so they can experience the added value for themselves. The content can take many forms. It can be:

1. Educational
2. Inspirational
3. Entertaining

And it doesn't necessarily need to include a promotional offer.

Let's look at an example: I don't have a specific drycleaner where I take my clothes. There are actually two drycleaners equidistant from my house. I just go to whichever one is on the way when I'm driving somewhere. But what if, on my next visit to one of these drycleaners, the person behind the counter asked me to sign up for his dry cleaner's e-newsletter, in which he sends out a tip for getting out specific types of stains once a week? That's something that would immediately add value to my life. I'd love that type of information, and it's not something I regularly seek out. In fact, if I got an email about, say, getting rid of spaghetti stains on clothing, I'd probably share it with my wife and friends who have kids. Why? Because the content is compelling. It's helping me solve a frequent problem: my son has spaghetti stains on his shirt pretty often, and this is how the experts recommend removing those stains. Solving a problem is a great way to provide someone with an experience worth sharing.

Here's another example: many realtors are great at providing value to potential customers through their marketing communications.

There's a realtor in my neighborhood who routinely sends out lists of the nearby homes on the market and those that have just sold. By doing this, she establishes herself as a housing expert within our community. Once a month I get an update about local housing prices, and she gets a valuable potential consumer touch point. That's a win-win situation. Making me feel smarter about the real estate market in my neighborhood gives me a great experience. And a good topic of conversation at our next block party.

The Honor Flight Network

Let's look at an example from one of my favorite non-profit organizations, The Honor Flight Network. The Honor Flight Network provides World War II veterans with an all-expenses paid trip to Washington, DC to visit the recently-finished WWII memorial. My grandfather was in the Navy during WWII. His ship, the USS Pennsylvania, was torpedoed in the last days of the war, but he survived. (Famous comedian Johnny Carson also served on the USS Pennsylvania.) About a year before my grandfather passed away, he was fortunate enough to go on an Honor Flight, and he loved every minute of it. He went with my Uncle, his step-son, who also served in the military.

Before the trip, leaders of the Honor Flight Network (via communications with my Uncle) invited us to write letters to my grandfather, in which we thanked him for his service. We sent our letters to a PO Box before the flight. While on the airplane home from Washington DC, the Honor Flight included "Mail Call," in which leaders of the Honor Flight distributed the letters to all of the WWII veterans. My wife and I sent in a letter along with a picture (shown on the next page).

Now, I come from a family of teachers. We have more than 20(!) on my dad's side alone. One of my other uncles invited all of his students to write letters to my grandfather as well. And boy did they listen. When it came time to distribute the letters on the flight home, one of the leaders approached my grandfather and uncle and told them there was a problem with the mail they received for him — there was simply too much mail, and they didn't want to make the other veterans feel bad for only receiving a few letters each. They wanted to give my grandfather the mail privately after landing. The trip leaders had never seen anything like this. He had literally received hundreds of letters of support from my family and their students. After returning home, my grandfather spent hours reading all the letters and he was so thankful for receiving them. A year later, for my grandfather's funeral, I compiled all the letters into a commemorative book.

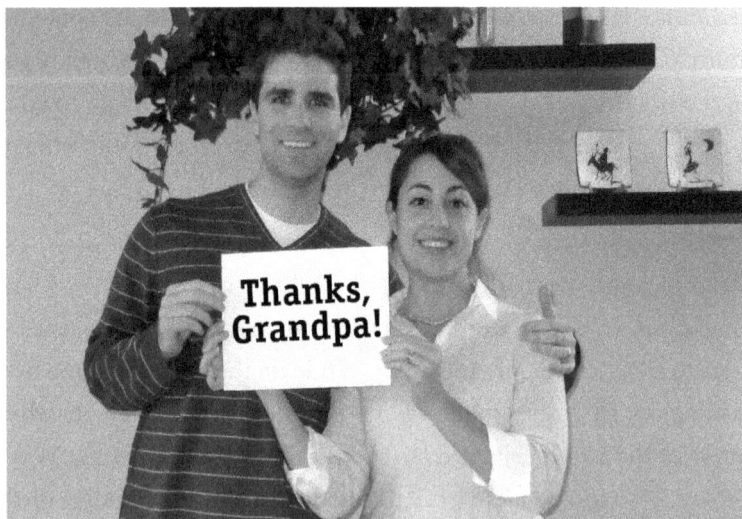

My wife and me honoring my grandfather.

While I wasn't able to attend the Honor Flight with my grandfather, I was able to share in his day through the Mail Call program. By asking our family to provide letters, we felt like we were a part of my grandfather's experience. What a truly amazing way to get a community of people involved with each veteran's journey. In a way, asking for input from family members is a marketing communication program for the Honor Flight Network. It so profoundly impacted my grandfather and me that I have made financial donations to the organization in his memory.

But let me be clear: the Honor Flight Network does not do the Mail Call program to increase donations. It does it to give each veteran an amazing experience — an experience I'm sharing with you now, and one that you may even share with people you know.

That's remarkable.

Remarkable Advertising — A Holey Postcard

Traditional advertising doesn't have to be boring. When done well, it can even be remarkable and worth telling a friend about. Consider an example from the wonderful world of direct mail advertising:

In the summer after I graduated college, I created a direct mail campaign that earned a whopping 15% response rate just by punching some holes in a postcard. (The average response rate for a direct mail campaign is under 2%.)

I was trying to pick up freelance graphic design work with local non-profits. So, I identified 20 prospective clients nearby and then designed the postcard on the next page. The headline read, "Are there holes in your advertising and design plans?" And I actually punched two big holes in the postcard, represented by the circles filled with black. I did my research and knew the post office would still deliver the cards with holes in those strategic spots.

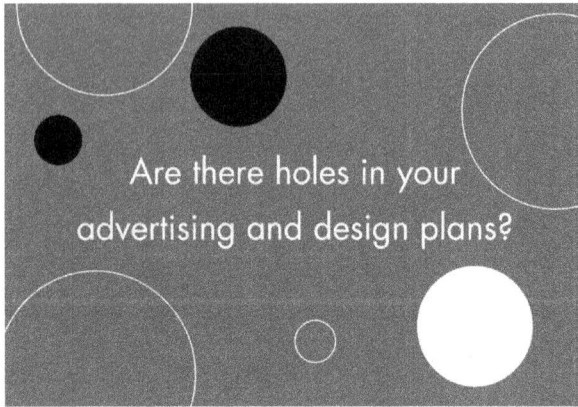

The holey postcard.

A few days after mailing the cards, I received calls from three of the non-profits. After a week, I was working for two of them. The holey postcard certainly grabbed attention. The first person who called me after receiving the card gushed about how cool the holes in the postcard were. He was convinced I hand delivered it and had not mailed it. Needless to say, he was impressed with my creative approach and wanted me to work for him.

Promotional Offers Worth Sharing

There are many ways to create remarkable promotional offers. Consider a traditional couponing strategy: A traditional coupon prompts one person to redeem a coupon for a one-time discount. If the discount offered is good enough, I suppose someone might tell her friends about it. But that would have to be a really great offer.

What if there was a different type of coupon that was inherently remarkable? For example, what if you've just opened your own yoga studio, and you offer a coupon that can only be redeemed by at least two people at a time? The coupon is for 15% off the first class for two people, and it's not valid for just one person. If you bring in three people, each of the three people will receive 20% off. Bring in four people and they each receive 25% off, and so on. That coupon would definitely be remarkable because a person would have to tell her friends about it, otherwise she wouldn't get a discount. That's a great way to get people talking about your yoga studio and a great way to get a lot of people to try your service. And what a great experience — you get to have fun with a whole bunch of your friends as a result of this piece of marketing communication. This example demonstrates a marketing communication tactic that is both remarkable and sharable, which is the second part of creating sharable messages.

Enabling Sharing

The second aspect of creating sharable experiences is enabling the sharing of those experiences. Just as creating compelling content is not only about creating a viral YouTube video, enabling the sharing of great experiences is not just about posting messages to online social networks. That is just one of many ways to help your target market share their experiences, and it may or may not be the best one.

There are countless ways to enable the sharing of a great experience provided by your marketing communication efforts. They can be as simple as enabling a "share this page" button on your website or encouraging customers to forward along your e-newsletter to anyone who might be interested. Include a business card with anything you ship, so your customer can give one to a friend if someone asks where she bought it. Give customers a referral bonus for recommending your monthly service to a friend.

Andy Sernovitz, author of the wonderful word-of-mouth marketing blog, "Damn I Wish I'd Thought of That," often writes that the best way to get a customer to share about an experience someone has had with your business is to simply ask her to do so. Think about that for a minute: all you have to do is ask. That doesn't cost anything at all. For example, if you own a hair salon, consider encouraging your customers to rate you on Yelp when they get home. While they're paying at the counter, give them a sticker or a business card that encourages them to do so. This is a great way for a business with a physical location to get online recommendations.

Or, if you're a tech startup with a great app, email your users two weeks after they download the app and invite them to rate it on their phone's app store. (Side note: Never create a fake review because that's slimy and could actually be illegal in the United States depending on how far you take it.) Simply invite your users to provide their genuine thoughts on your product in a way that can be read by others. At the end of this book, I'm going to ask you to share the book with your friends. It's that easy.

Now, let's revisit the topic of social media platforms for a minute. If your target market consists of heavy social media users, you should consider using social media channels as a way to enable the sharing of the experiences you have provided them. While some noted marketers like Don Schultz, the outspoken former chair of Northwestern's Integrated Marketing Communications program and a former professor of mine in graduate school, would argue that social media is best for listening and not shouting marketing messages at consumers, I'd argue there's a way to balance both enticing customers to share about their experiences with you and listening to (and politely responding to) customer feedback. Social media offers brands a very easy way to enable customers to share about their brand experiences, making it a very attractive platform on which to do so.

Summary

There are endless ways to get existing customers to tell people about your product or services. And if you create experiences worth sharing, there are plenty of ways to encourage people who are new to your brand to give you a try. That's why, no matter what your marketing tactics, after choosing the right target market, you must prioritize creating compelling experiences and giving customers a way to tell their friends about you.

One final disappointing note about the SpanAir example cited at the beginning of this chapter: unfortunately, not too many years after its great, share-worthy Christmas Eve event, SpanAir went out of business. But it wasn't because of poor marketing communications; the airline was riddled with financial problems. Although they are not nearly as fun and interesting, there are actually more aspects to running a successful business than just providing awesome experiences and having great marketing communications. And SpanAir fell short in those areas.

chapter 4
prioritize based on ROMI

After prioritizing marketing tactics that reach your target market and creating shareable experiences, you're well on your way to success. There's one final aspect you need to consider when prioritizing marketing communication tactics: return on marketing investment, or ROMI.

ROMI is the amount of revenue a marketing campaign brings in, minus the amount it costs to produce. It can be expressed as a dollar amount: "this campaign brought in a return of $3,000;" or a percentage: "I spent $1,000 on this campaign and earned $2,000, so my ROMI is 100% (calculation: [$2,000 − $1,000]/$1,000)."

There are several building blocks to measuring ROMI. You should start by measuring the immediate impact of a marketing communication tactic. An example would be: "I spent $50 to send this email to my email subscriber list, and I received $500 in donations as a result." That's called a *direct financial outcome.*

Eventually, you should also work to measure the indirect financial outcomes of your marketing communications. This means measuring things that don't have direct financial outcomes but are still important to your marketing initiatives. An example would be the number of followers you have on a social media site. Over time, the combination of direct and indirect financial outcomes will lead to an overall measure of the lifetime value of each customer.

Direct Financial Outcomes

The easiest way to measure the return on your marketing investment is to look at the revenue generated by the piece of marketing communication your customers came into contact directly prior to making a purchase or donation. Said another way, if a marketing communication tactic was the final impetus for a consumer to make a purchase, that's considered a direct financial outcome. Examples would include a customer clicking on an online ad and then purchasing a product on your website, a customer purchasing something from your booth at a trade show, and someone donating to your cause via the special envelope you included in your direct mail campaign.

You should always prioritize the types of marketing communications that cause measurable, direct financial outcomes. It's the easiest way to prove the value of your marketing investments and with limited resources, it's important to prioritize these so-called "direct-response" tactics.

Indirect Financial Outcomes

There are many different valuable customer touch points that do not produce direct financial outcomes. However, it's important to attribute value to these touch points as you build a complete understanding of the value of your marketing investments. To do so, you first need to identify the behaviors worth measuring as a result of your marketing communications. Look at any action you want consumers to take or actions that you value. While different for every organization, examples include:

- Number of email newsletter subscribers
- Time spent on website
- Number of Twitter followers
- Number of unique website visitors

- Number of mobile app downloads
- Number of in-store visitors
- Number of special event attendees
- Number of Facebook page interactions
- Time spent watching YouTube videos per viewer
- Number of blog comments

Each of these consumer behaviors are a direct result of your marketing communications, but may not immediately lead to increased sales. They are mini-acquisitions that may eventually lead to purchases. Eventually, you should work to correlate these indirect financial outcomes with sales. You should know the approximate value of each of them. If you don't know the value, you should start by making an educated guess and testing your hypothesis. Take an initial guess: maybe a newsletter sign-up is worth 0.5% of an average-sized order. When in doubt, guess a really small number, like lower than 1%.

Let's look at an example based on some numbers. For this example, assume that you have $500 to invest in a marketing campaign that you expect could yield one of these three results:

Outcome	Purchase conversion rate	Average order size	Revenue
1. 2,500 new email newsletter subscribers	0.5%	$200	$2,500
2. 10,000 new Twitter followers	0.25%	$200	$5,000
3. 60 phone calls received	10.0%	$200	$1,200

In the example above, if you know your average customer order size ($200) and conversion rates (defined as the number of people in the first column who will actually make a purchase), which aren't too hard to figure out or at least estimate, you can put a value on many different micro-conversions.

So how do you use this information? If you think you can invest $500 in a marketing campaign that increases your number of Twitter followers by 10,000, you could justify doing it because you will bring in $5,000 in new revenue, based on this example. It would also be worth investing in campaigns to produce the other two outcomes, since they produce a great return on investment, too. If you were forced to make a decision on which campaign to invest in first, you would prioritize the one that brings in the most money — the campaign to increase the number of your Twitter followers.

Understanding the value of a mini-acquisition helps attribute value to all the indirect financial outcomes your marketing communications produce. But in the example above, we only looked at the average value of a single customer purchase ($200). The final step to measuring the return on your marketing investments is to measure the lifetime value of a customer — taking into consideration all of her purchases over time.

A Note About Customer Lifetime Value

As you are increasingly able to measure ROMI on direct and indirect financial outcomes, you should work toward combining these measures into one holistic measure of customer lifetime value (CLV). Your goal is to identify the value each customer brings to your business and then focus your marketing communication efforts on targeting the segments of customers that are most valuable over their lifetime.

Knowing what a customer is worth will allow you to decide how much you can spend marketing to each customer. Many companies are able to identify a minimum required return on all investments and are then able to prioritize their entire budgets, including their marketing communication spend, on that required return.

To illustrate this point with a very simple example, let's say a tech startup has investors who demand at least double their money back. So, the minimum acceptable return on marketing investment would be two times the amount invested. If the tech company has a small revenue stream from a loyal customer base, it might calculate that its average CLV is $100, stemming from mobile application purchases over five years. Therefore, the marketing department cannot spend more than $50 to acquire that customer if it wants to hit the minimum ROI requirement set forth by its investors.

Of course, the above example is very basic. It doesn't take into account the time value of money — if a customer is worth $100 over a five-year lifetime, the customer's value today would need to be discounted. Check out other resources on discounted cash flows if you want to explore more advanced ways of thinking about CLV.

A Beginning Benchmark

A lot of startups, small businesses, and non-profits aren't sure what's a good return on their marketing investment when they're first getting started. Of course, ROMI varies widely by industry and marketing tactic, but if you twist my arm and ask for a benchmark, I'd recommend that you stay away from any tactic that has an ROMI of less than 2:1 at first. You should actually aim a lot higher in the beginning. Aim for tactics that have an ROMI of 10:1 or higher when you're just getting started.

How to Track the Outcomes of Your Marketing Communications

The first step in measuring ROMI is to track all of your marketing communications. First, you should create a list of all your marketing communications. Then, you should identify the desired outcomes that could stem from those communications. Finally, you should go about tying your marketing tactics to the desired results via tracking techniques. Examples include:

1. Include promotional codes on all coupons, promotional offers, and direct mail campaigns. When customers use the coupons, record the code in a database or spreadsheet.

2. Use web analytics such as Google Analytics (it's free!) to measure your online referrals (such as email messages, online advertising, and social media referrals) and track how people navigate your website. You can even see where in your purchase funnel people drop off.

3. Ask customers where they heard about your company on your online ordering form or when speaking to them on the phone. This aids in measuring marketing communications that are hard to measure, like radio ads, billboards, and TV commercials.

A Note About Cost

While it's great, in theory, to prioritize your marketing communications by return on investment, it's worth noting that for startups, small businesses, and non-profit organizations, cost is a big factor in these decisions, regardless of the promised return. Marketing budgets can be tiny — especially at startups, so it's very important to choose communication tactics that are free or very inexpensive and can be increased as performance is proven. You should prioritize marketing tactics that can be measured and directly tied your key performance indicators. Ideally, they should be tied to sales.

Consider the risk of making a large financial commitment to any form of marketing communication that requires a large upfront investment in production or media. Examples include running TV commercials or buying billboards. While the promise of reaching a large amount of people may be tempting with these mediums, consider the risk of such large, upfront investments without proving their worth. At small businesses, startups, and non-profits, you may not want to risk large portions of your marketing budget on these types of marketing communications. And always go back to the first rule of prioritizing marketing communications: focus on your target market.

Summary

Return on marketing investment comes down to increasing sales by more than you spend on your marketing investment. There are direct and indirect financial outcomes from all of your marketing communications. Those financial outcomes are the building blocks used to measure a customer's lifetime value.

It's important to prioritize your marketing communications based on their ROMI. Invest in tactics that produce a high return on marketing investment and refrain from investing in those that produce a low return.

chapter 5
putting it all together with a cool visual framework

In the previous three chapters, I gave you a lot of information to digest. Let's take a minute to pause, re-focus, and review the key themes from each one:

1. **Prioritize marketing communications that reach your target markets.** There are many ways to group customers into target markets, and you should choose the ways that work best for you. Frameworks I provided were searchers, passion markets, and trigger markets — if you don't have current customers or customer data — and RFM, and RFM+ models if you do.

2. **When investing in marketing communication tactics, prioritize those that provide an experience worth sharing and then enable people to share those experiences easily.** It's not just about creating the next viral sensation on YouTube or simply posting something to a social network. It's about creating content that is educational, inspirational, or entertaining and giving people ways to share it.

3. **Measure the indirect and direct financial outcomes of your marketing communications and prioritize the tactics that have the highest return on marketing investment.** Over time,

focus on developing ways to test and measure customer lifetime value and invest in the initiatives that produce the highest CLV.

Now that we've fully discussed these three factors for setting marketing communication priorites, the next step is to use them to prioritize your specific, tactical ideas. We'll do this with an easy-to-use visual framework that will actually show you in which tactics to invest and which ones to avoid.

Visual Framework

We are going to use all your marketing communication tactics and ideas to build a two-dimensional bubble chart. (The final chart can be seen on page 71 if you want a sneak peek to see where we're headed.) The chart is composed of three things:

1. **X-Axis: Target Market.** The degree to which a marketing communication tactic reaches your target market

2. **Y-Axis: Shareable Experiences.** The degree to which your marketing communications provide experiences worth sharing and are easily shareable.

3. **Size of Each Bubble: ROMI per Tactic.** The return on marketing investment for each tactic — both direct and indirect financial outcomes.

1. X-Axis: Target Market

Our x-axis is a spectrum based on two things we discussed in Chapter Two:

- The degree to which a marketing communication tactic reaches your target market

   and

- The degree to which someone is looking to buy what you sell

Somewhat targeted

Targeted broadly ———————————|——————————— Reaches target market
and/or looking to buy

TARGET MARKET

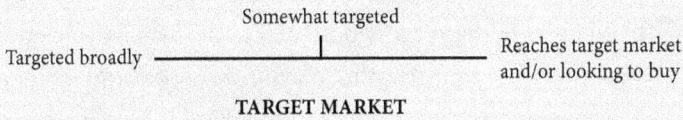

The furthest point on the left of the axis is labeled "Targeted broadly." Why not "Targeting everyone?" Well, because every marketing communication tactic has a target market. There's no such thing as "targeting everyone." For example, putting together a website inherently targets people with access to the Internet. TV ads only target people with TVs who are watching that program. And even though dropping fliers from a helicopter over Philadelphia seems like it's targeting everyone, it's actually only targeting people who are outdoors in Philadelphia at that very minute.

On the other hand, the furthest point on the right is labeled: "Reaches target market and/or looking to buy." Why this wording? Well, because we're incorporating our two factors here:

- *Reaches target market:* After you've successfully identified at least one target market based on passion markets, trigger markets, or RFM+, you should judge your potential marketing communication tactics based on whether or not you can reach that specific market. If you can, then you should plot that tactic with a dot at the right end of this spectrum. As an example, if you've identified a passion market of motorcycle enthusiasts from San Diego interested in old Indian motorcycles and are able to reach that exact target with a specific marketing communication tactic, that tactic should be plotted on the far right of this axis.

- *Looking to buy:* Your best potential customer is one who is looking for the products or services you sell, or looking to support your charitable cause. These customers are the proverbial "low-hanging fruit." They are the easiest customers to convert. Perhaps these potential customers have been to your store or your website, and maybe those of your competitors, but have not made a purchase decision yet. They have searched for your product or brand name on their favorite search engine and are still debating about when, where, or how to purchase or donate. Regardless of whether or not this person meets your target market qualifications in terms of demographics or other characteristics, this "searcher" should be your top target.

We'll call the middle point of the x-axis "somewhat targeted." This descriptor is intentionally vague. It allows room for you to define the minimum threshold for a marketing communication tactic to reach your target market. Continuing the Indian motorcycle example from above: if you're only able to reach motorcycle enthusiasts from California (and not just San Diego) with a marketing tactic, I would consider that "somewhat targeted." Similarly, if you were only able to reach Indian motorcycle enthusiasts on the West coast, I'd also consider that marketing tactic to be "somewhat targeted," and you would plot that tactic in the middle of this axis.

2. Y-Axis: Shareable Experiences

Our y-axis is a spectrum measuring two things that you've heard referenced many times:

- The degree to which your marketing communications create experiences worth sharing
  and
- The degree to which those experiences are easy to share

Because there are two aspects to this spectrum, you need to consider each one independently of the other and then combine your assessment of each into one point on the chart.

Experiences Worth Sharing

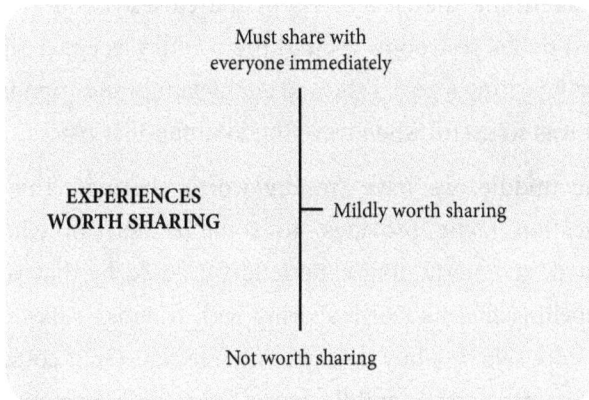

```
                    Must share with
                  everyone immediately

                         │
                         │
                         │
   EXPERIENCES           │
   WORTH SHARING       ──┤   Mildly worth sharing
                         │
                         │

                   Not worth sharing
```

The furthest point on the bottom of this portion of the y-axis is labeled, "not worth sharing." The label is, again, intentionally vague and up for your interpretation. Marketing communications that don't provide educational, inspirational, or entertaining experiences fall here. So do advertisements that provide no value at all to a consumer base. If your messages are just shouting your brand name at a customer, they fall to the bottom of this spectrum. For example, slapping your logo on a billboard near the airport without any other messaging, value proposition, or call to action would be plotted at the bottom of the y-axis in this spectrum.

On the other hand, the highest point on this spectrum is called, "must share with everyone immediately." That's how customers feel when seeing the most hilarious, educational, and inspirational content. That content doesn't feel like marketing. It's the type of content that makes a person laugh incredibly hard at something and then tell all her friends, family, and coworkers about it. It's something so thought-provoking that it inspires someone to share her newfound knowledge with everyone she knows. One of my favorite examples of share-worthy content in recent memory came from Charmin toilet paper, of all places. The brand created a mobile app called "Sit or Go" that enabled users to determine the cleanliness of the closest public restrooms. Users rated public restrooms around the country as either sit-worthy or not worth visiting ("go"). I showed all my family and friends the app because it was so useful when traveling to unfamiliar places.

In the middle, we have "mildly worth sharing." This type of communication tactic provides, to some extent, an educational, inspirational, or entertaining experience. It could be that your offer is so compelling that it's worth sharing with friends — like a 50% off an entire store sale or a buy one, get one free sale. Or, it could be that one of your initiatives is mildly funny, sexy, or informative. A few people will share your message with their friends, but not everybody will; and nobody is going to bust their gut laughing at your message or shed a tear from an emotional response to your communication. It's just average.

Experiences That Are Easy to Share

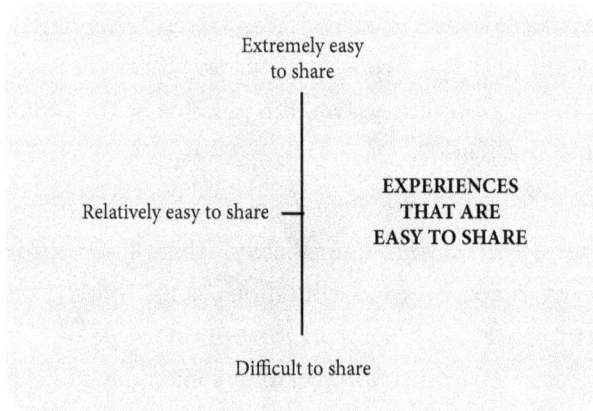

Extremely easy
to share

Relatively easy to share —

**EXPERIENCES
THAT ARE
EASY TO SHARE**

Difficult to share

The furthest point on the bottom of this portion of the y-axis is labeled, "difficult to share." Why not, "impossible to share"? Because you can tell a friend about anything. Sure, it may be hard to describe what you saw, heard, tasted, or felt, but you can try. It's not impossible to share anything. However, something like a radio commercial you heard while driving to work is hard to play for a friend to hear. Unless you were recording it while you were in the car, the chances of it being found anywhere else, like on a website, are very slim. (There's a free business idea for my lucky readers: a website that gathers all radio ads and enables them to be shared more easily.) Print ads and billboards are hard to share because they require you to either cut them out (print ads) or take a picture (billboards) to show someone else.

On the other hand, the highest point on this axis is called, "extremely easy to share." These types of communications are inherently shareable because sharing is built into them. Anything posted to a social network is easy to like, share, +1, pin, tweet, email, etc. Often times, online communications will be automatically shared with your friends if you allow them to be, which is truly the definition of "extremely easy to share."

Finally, the middle point on this portion of the y-axis is called "relatively easy to share." Printed coupons handed out on a street corner are relatively easy to share because you can just hand one to somebody else or post one on the refrigerator in the break room at work. The sharing isn't done on your behalf, but it's relatively easy to share. As another example, attending a trade show as an exhibitor makes it relatively easy to share your message with the people who will walk by your booth because they are a receptive audience and may tell their friends about what they heard.

Combining the Two Y-Axis Measures

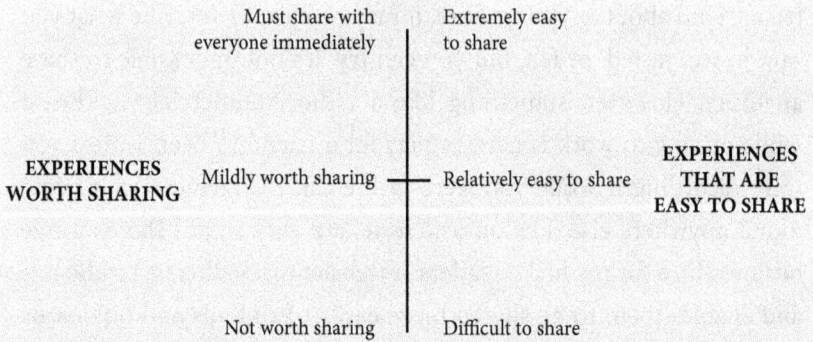

Must share with everyone immediately | Extremely easy to share

EXPERIENCES WORTH SHARING — Mildly worth sharing — Relatively easy to share — **EXPERIENCES THAT ARE EASY TO SHARE**

Not worth sharing | Difficult to share

Plotting a marketing communication tactic along the y-axis requires you to combine both measures into one metric. You have to judge the degree to which the tactic provides an experience worth sharing and the degree to which it is easy to share. If your tactic is extremely easy to share but not very compelling, then it falls somewhere in the middle of the axis. Similarly, if you create a marketing communication tactic that provides an extremely compelling experience but it's not very easy to share, it also belongs somewhere in the middle of the axis.

Plotting Tactics

Combining the x- and y-axes gives us the following chart:

Easy to share &
must share with
everyone immediately

Targeted broadly

Reaches target market
and/or looking to buy

Difficult to share &
not worth sharing

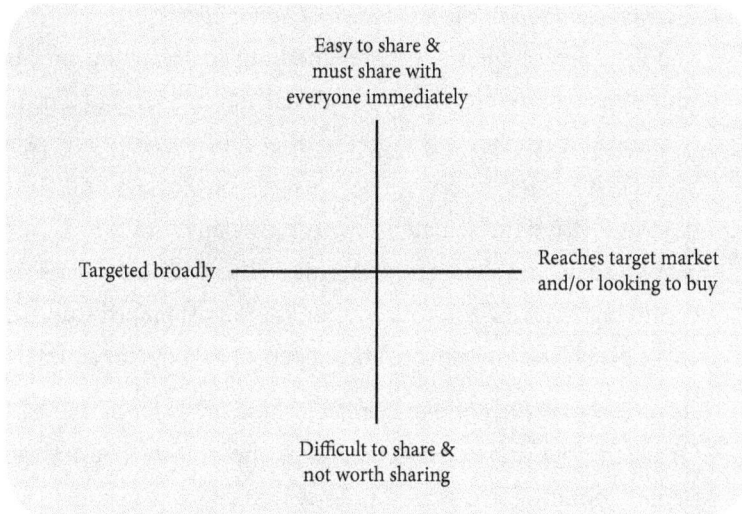

Now it's time to plot on the chart each marketing communication tactic you are currently using or thinking of using. Plot each tactic according to the guidelines we've already established for each axis.

Let's go back to an example we used in the Preface and plot a few example marketing communication tactics for our family-friendly pizzeria. We identify one of our hypothetical target markets as parents age 35-50 in the surrounding neighborhood looking for a quick and easy dinner solution, especially on Friday and Saturday nights. We will consider four potential marketing communication tactics:

- *Hiring a man in a gorilla costume to distribute fliers in front of the restaurant.*
  If the pizzeria gets a lot of foot traffic during the day, this could be a good way to target the surrounding community, but it's tough to reach only our target demographic. It could work fairly well to attract people on Fridays and Saturdays. A flier can be shared fairly easily, and a gorilla suit is something someone may tell her friends about.

- *Placing a coupon in the local printed newspaper.*
  The local newspaper is a better medium for reaching the surrounding community than a national newspaper, but I'm not convinced it reaches our target market more so than any other market. It could, however, reach people on Fridays and Saturdays and drive immediate sales. A newspaper coupon is fairly easy to share if it's cut out. It's remarkable if it's for a large discount, but a run-of-the-mill coupon is pretty standard stuff. This tactic doesn't do anything to attract people looking for a pizzeria.

- *Advertising on the Internet against local searches for pizzerias.*
  Of all the options listed here, this is the one that best targets people looking for a pizzeria. As search engines become more and more social — providing results recommended by your social graph — they are moving toward becoming shareable.

- *Sponsoring a pizza night at a local school's Parent Teacher Association meeting.*
  This tactic likely reaches our precise target market in terms of the demographic. But while free pizza is pretty cool, it may not be all that remarkable. If the pizzeria handed out coupons at the meeting, that may inspire some people to share about the pizza. Overall, this might be a case of the right market but not a very shareable experience.

The above four tactics are just examples and don't reflect my opinion about these tactics in every marketing situation. Also, you'll note that I'm using a lot of advertising tactics in these examples. I'm doing so just because they are easy for everyone to envision. I'm in no way saying that the only marketing communication tactics worth considering involve advertising.

Continuing the example, I've plotted the above four tactics on the following graph.

Easy to share &
must share with
everyone immediately

Gorilla Costume •

**Search
Engines**

Targeted broadly

• Reaches target market
and/or looking to buy

Newspaper Coupon •

•
**PTA
Sponsorship**

Difficult to share &
not worth sharing

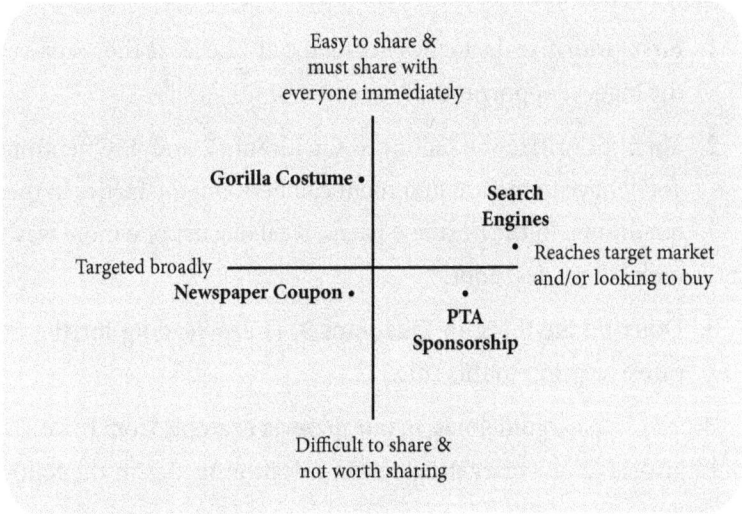

Now that I've plotted our potential marketing communication tactics, we can prioritize each tactic.

Prioritizing Tactics on the Chart

To prioritize our marketing communication tactics, we'll divide our chart into four quadrants, as you see here:

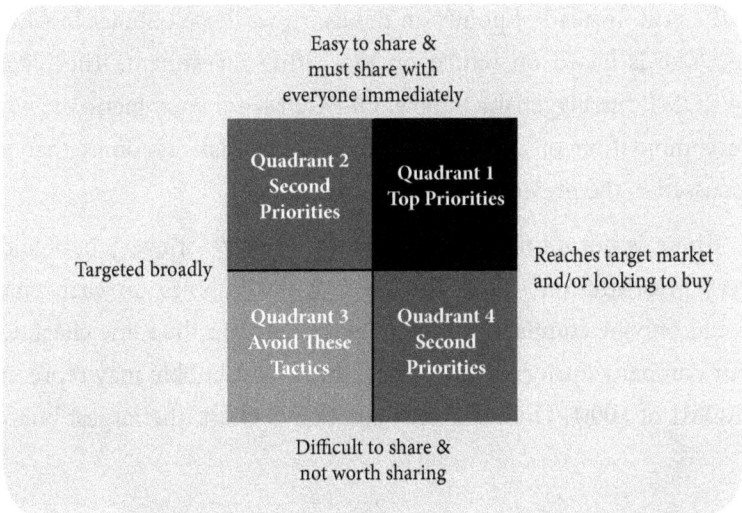

Easy to share &
must share with
everyone immediately

**Quadrant 2
Second
Priorities**

**Quadrant 1
Top Priorities**

Targeted broadly

Reaches target market
and/or looking to buy

**Quadrant 3
Avoid These
Tactics**

**Quadrant 4
Second
Priorities**

Difficult to share &
not worth sharing

We prioritize tactics in this order:

1. First, prioritize the tactics in Quadrant 1 because they represent the biggest opportunities for success.

2. Then, prioritize the tactics in Quadrants 2 and 4. Oftentimes, you'll have to make a judgment call between the tactics in these quadrants. In the next few pages, we'll discuss one more way to make these decisions.

3. Don't do anything in Quadrant 3. (Keep reading for the one rare exception to this rule.)

Based on these guidelines, in our pizzeria example from before, we would prioritize our marketing communication tactics in the following way:

1. Advertising against searches

2. Gorilla costume and PTA sponsorship

3. Avoid: Newspaper coupon

3. Size of Each Bubble: ROMI per Tactic

The third and final aspect of our chart is the size of each tactic's point on the grid. Instead of points on the chart, we'll use bubbles in which their size is based on return on marketing investment. The bigger the ROMI, the bigger the bubble. Our ROMI for each tactic includes the combination of direct and indirect financial outcomes that we discussed in the previous chapter.

There is not a universal formula for the size of every bubble on every prioritization chart. The sizes of the bubbles on each chart should only be compared to the other bubbles on the same chart. On your company's prioritization chart, the largest bubble may represent a ROMI of 100:1. On a different company's chart, the largest bubble may represent a ROMI of 5:1. The point is that the size of each bubble should only be compared to those on the same chart and not to those on other charts.

Given this final component of our chart, our official order for prioritizing tactics on the graph is:

1. First, prioritize the marketing communication tactics with the highest ROMI, regardless of quadrant — even in the rare event that the tactic falls in Quadrant 3.

If you don't know ROMI or you have tactics with the same ROMI:

2. Prioritize the tactics in Quadrant 1.

3. Then, prioritize the tactics in Quadrants 2 and 4.

4. Don't do anything in Quadrant 3. These are not worth pursuing, given the rest of the opportunities.

Let's look at one final example to show how ROMI impacts the look of our prioritization chart.

One Final Example

Say you're a startup that makes a mobile application that assists with travel planning. It's free to download and use a basic version, but users can pay a small sum of money (like $2) for enhanced app features. Several thousand people have already downloaded the app, so you know approximately what a download is worth to you. You can use that number to calculate an estimated ROMI for each marketing tactic you are considering.

One trigger market you've thought of comprises tech-savvy business professionals who have recently started new jobs in which they will need to travel a lot. Therefore, they are heavy mobile app users. We will consider four potential marketing communication tactics to target this market and achieve new downloads:

- *In-app advertising across a network of other mobile applications.*
  Some of the best potential app downloaders are those who are already using mobile apps, so this type of advertising could be quite promising. It certainly targets heavy app users, and with a little bit of targeting layered on top, it's likely that you may be able to reach a set of mobile app users quite similar to your target. This type of advertising isn't very remarkable and it's not very easy to share. However, this advertising provides a great ROMI in this hypothetical situation.

- *Place billboards featuring quick response (QR) codes inside public trains in three large, metropolitan cities.*
  The direct-response aspect of this solution is good and could be remarkable among friends commuting together. However, if we are trying to target frequent travelers, they may not be commuting on the train very frequently. Also, this solution requires a large capital commitment upfront, limiting the ROMI.

- *Creating Facebook mobile ads to promote app downloads.*
  Social networks are, well, inherently social. Facebook also provides great targeting options that will help us get pretty close to our target market. And since the ads are targeting people on mobile devices, that's great, too. This option provides a nice ROMI.

- *Creating a compelling video of how to use the app and posting it on YouTube.*
  Assuming you've done a great job optimizing the video and its description so it can be found easily on YouTube, this could be a great way to get the message out about your app. It's easy to share an online video. There are some costs involved with creating a video, so the ROMI isn't quite as high as other options here.

Easy to share &
must share with
everyone immediately

**YT
Video**

**FB
Ads**

Billboards

Targeted broadly — Reaches target market
and/or looking to buy

**In-App
Ads**

Difficult to share &
not worth sharing

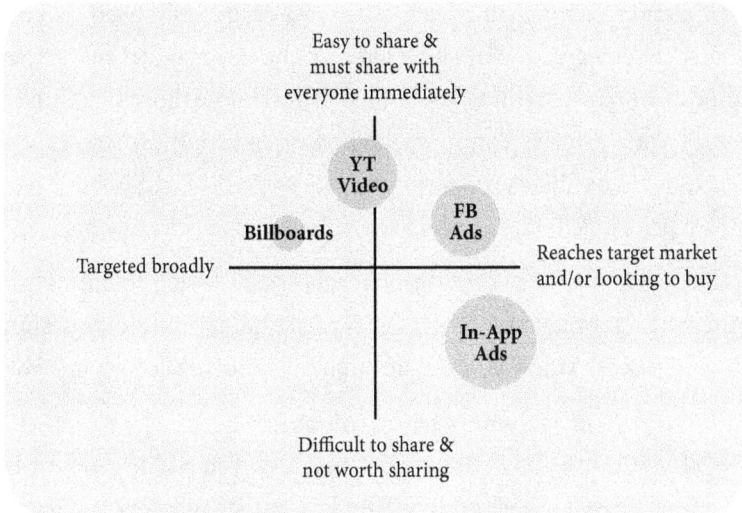

Since we have hypothetical ROMI information on these four tactics, we know exactly how to prioritize these tactics:

1. In-App advertisements — they have the highest ROMI, so they are prioritized first, even though they are in Quadrant 4.

2. Facebook advertisements — this tactic and the YouTube tactic have the same ROMI, but since Facebook ads fall in Quadrant 1, they get the priority here.

3. Posting a compelling YouTube video — this tactic has the same ROMI as the Facebook ads and should therefore get priority over its Quadrant 2 roommate.

4. Lastly, prioritize the billboards since they have the lowest ROMI.

What if you don't know one of the three elements to this chart?

If you're working at a startup and haven't had any customers yet, there's a good chance you don't have enough information about our three prioritization factors. But that's okay. You really only need to know the first two: degree to which a tactic reaches your target market and degree to which something is sharable. If you know those two, you can identify your priority communication tactics simply by the location of each tactic on the chart — not the size of the ROMI bubble. This is how we prioritized our tactics in the pizzeria example a few pages ago.

But, you may have additional questions when building this framework for your own business. Here are a few common questions that you may ask when working through this prioritization framework:

- *What if I don't know my target markets?*
  If you don't know your target markets, you need to revisit the first three ways I proposed finding target markets in Chapter Two: 1.) identify people searching for you and your products or causes, 2.) passion markets, and 3.) trigger markets. You need to work harder at identifying target markets because it's impossible to target everybody. If you're trying to target everybody, you'll end up targeting nobody.

- *How do I predict the degree to which an experience will be shared?*
  Nobody can predict a viral marketing sensation. No matter what anybody tells you, absolutely nobody is able to say with certainty that your marketing campaign will be shared by millions of people. There are many marketers in this world trying to create the next smash hit everyday, but it's not easy to do and prior success doesn't guarantee future success.

What you *can* do to best predict whether or not something provides a compelling experience worth sharing is test your messages with your markets to see what resonates. Then enable tools for sharing. This is one part science and one part art. You can ask friends and family for their honest feedback as a starting point. Err on the conservative side and assume not as many people as you initially think will share something you create.

If you are really having a tough time figuring out if your content is worth sharing, then it probably isn't. Focus on the tools you will provide to customers to share your content. Then go back and create some content worth sharing.

- *Many of the tactics I'm considering are either worth sharing or easy to share, but not both. Don't those cancel each other out on the y-axis?*
  You should prioritize tactics that are both worth sharing and easy to share. But you may find that most of the tactics you are considering seem to cancel each other out because of the combined two y-axis measures, causing the tactics to land mostly in the middle of the y-axis. If that's the case, put more of an emphasis on prioritizing tactics that are worth sharing and place less of an emphasis on those that are easy to share. It's easier to add methods of shareability to a tactic than it is to make a tactic worth sharing.

- *Should I use one chart per target market?*
  If you're a startup or just beginning to think about marketing communications, you should plot all of your marketing communications options on just one chart. The place in which you plot each tactic on the chart will reflect that tactic's ability to reach one or more of your target markets.

As you become more advanced in your marketing communications, I recommend that you try to create one prioritization chart for each of your target markets. You can prioritize which chart to focus on first by ranking them by the ROMI you expect to receive from each target market.

Summary

The best way to prioritize your marketing communication tactics is to plot each one on a chart so you can see the impact each one will make on your business. The chart comprises all that we've discussed in the previous three chapters: reaching your target market, creating shareable experiences, and achieving a high return on marketing investment. After plotting each tactic, you should first prioritize the tactics with the highest ROMI. If you don't know the ROMI on each tactic or several are the same, begin prioritizing tactics that reach your target markets and are shareable. You should skip any tactics that don't reach your target markets and aren't worth sharing. As you become more advanced at prioritizing, you should begin creating a chart for each target market you are trying to reach.

chapter 6
the five must-haves

Now that we have walked through the three most important ways to determine how to set marketing communication priorities and how they relate to each other, it's worth noting that there are some elements of your marketing communications plan that are so fundamental they don't even need to be plotted on a chart.

These five tactics are must-haves for all startups, small businesses, and non-profits. In fact, they are so essential that you shouldn't even consider other tactics unless you have these five in place. If you have an extremely limited marketing budget and can only afford to do a few things, you should do the following five things in the order in which I present them. Maybe I should have started the book with these five tactics, but I thought it was important to lay the groundwork for how to set priorities before outlining any specific marketing tactics. Perhaps I have a prioritization problem of my own.

The five marketing communication tactics you must execute in order to achieve success are:

1. Utilize your physical location if you have a brick-and-mortar presence

2. Build and maintain a website

3. Offer customers a way to speak to someone at your business or non-profit

4. Be found by your target markets

5. Offer at least one engaging way for customers to build a community and interact with your brand

Let's discuss each one of these:

1. Utilize Your Physical Location

If you have a physical location, you have certainly invested a lot of money in it. In order to squeeze the value out of this investment, you must take advantage of all the marketing communication opportunities it provides:

- You need a sign out front that's easy to read and tells people the name of your business and what you do.

- If you have a lot of traffic (by foot, car, or any other means) outside your space, you need to post signs about special offers or give free samples.

- Inside your space, consider what you want your customers to pay attention to. Don't overwhelm them with signs about a dozen different specials or products, but consider featuring one new item or one monthly promotion via a sign or on a tv screen.

As an example, the church I attend is located on a popular corner in Aurora, IL — a suburb of Chicago. We realized very quickly that the best way to get the word out about special events at the church was to install permanent posts on the corner of our property so that we could hang vinyl banners advertising the events. So every time we want to advertise events like Christmas services or our annual helicopter-dropped Easter egg hunt, we pay a local print shop $100 to print a vinyl banner advertising the event, and we hang the banner on the permanently-installed posts. Thousands of cars drive by the church and the banner every day, giving us plenty of exposure to the local community in advance of the events.

Movie theaters are great at advertising what films they are playing. Most will put the names of the movies in big letters outside of the theater so all who walk or drive by are informed. Think of your physical location like movie theaters do — as an opportunity to advertise your businesses in bright lights.

2. Build and Maintain a Website

According to Google, nearly 60% of small businesses don't have a website. That's a shame because a website is a very inexpensive way to communicate with existing and potential customers in which you, as a marketer, have a lot of control over the messaging on the site. You can decide your domain name, the look-and-feel of the site, and what content to feature. And it's available 24 hours a day, 7 days a week to engage customers when they want to be engaged, answer their questions, and help them make informed buying decisions.

If you don't have a website, there are plenty of resources for helping you get one quickly and affordably. Sites like GoDaddy.com and Google's Get Your Business Online will help you with the entire process from registering a domain name to building and publishing your first site.

At a minimum, you need to include your business or non-profit's contact information, a description of your products and services, and a call to action on the site. If you can include customer testimonials via text or video, those work really well, too. Pictures go a long way online, if that's appropriate for your organization, so don't be afraid to include them instead of long passages of text.

But, you don't have to create a standard, run-of-the-mill site. You can get creative. Two of my favorite websites in terms of their creativity are:

- Ad agency Boone Oakley simply has a series of interactive YouTube videos as its website. It's very clever and certainly shows off how creative the firm is. You should Google it. It's cool.

- Skittles actually turned its website over to its fans and simply featured a live stream of its Twitter account on its site. It was a risky move, but it was really engaging and definitely shareable.

Once you have your website up and running, it's important to keep it updated frequently. How frequently? That's tough to say, but I'd recommend updating something on your site at least once per month. You need to give customers a reason to come back to your site, keeping you at the top of their mind. Ideas for keeping it updated include:

- Update a Frequently Asked Questions page with new questions as you get them.

- Add a weekly deal or special.

- Include a monthly update from your company president (but don't make it boring).

- Recap events that have happened recently and advertise upcoming events.

- Ask for customer or donor testimonials and post them on your site. Or simply allow customers to post their own reviews on your site.

Taking your website to the next level requires installing an analytics package to the site, measuring key performance indicators, and making business decisions based on the analytics. There are several analytic packages you can put on your site like Omniture, WebTrends, and Google Analytics. Google Analytics is free and easy to install, so I'd recommend starting there.

There are many resources online and in print all about online measurement for beginners through experts. The foremost expert in the topic, though, is Avinash Kaushik (who I'm honored to say wrote the foreword to this book). If you'd like more information about this topic, I recommend Googling his name and reading his thoughts.

3. A Way to Speak to Someone at Your Company or Non-Profit

Customer service is not dead. And nothing will ever replace the opportunity for great customer service provided by person-to-person conversations. It will always be very important for businesses and non-profits of all sizes to offer customers and potential customers the ability to speak to someone at their organization. There's just no way to replace the human element of conducting business or raising donations.

Now, the ways in which you can choose to engage in conversations with your customers are constantly evolving and the available options will likely increase even more in the next few years. Consider these three options:

- A traditional phone line

- Video conferencing via services like Skype and Google+ Hangouts

- Instant messaging via computer or text messaging via mobile device (offering these services in addition to the option to call would be best, I'd say)

A phone call can provide customers with an experience they can only receive when interacting with a real person. They can receive empathy when something has gone wrong or enthusiasm when excited about an upcoming event. They can even find relief when in a tough situation. My favorite story about the impact a phone call with a company can have has been repeated time and time again, but I'm going to include it again here. Tony Hsieh, the CEO of online retailer Zappos likes to tell this story:

One night, Mr. Hsieh and some vendors returned to a hotel room late at night. Someone in the group was craving pizza but was unfortunately told room service had ended for the evening. As a joke, Mr. Hsieh suggested calling the Zappos customer service line to find a place for food. Even though Zappos doesn't sell pizza, the vendor called Zappos' customer service line and the representative found a list of local pizza places that would deliver to the hotel. The vendor was extremely grateful. He had a story to share for a long time, and it was all made possible because Zappos has a great customer service program through its call center.

4. Be Found by Your Target Markets

In Chapter Two, we discussed the importance of the searchers — the people who are actively looking for your products or services or to support your cause. That's why it's important to be found by these searchers. Being found really boils down to two things:

1. Being found online

2. Being found in-person (or "offline") if you have a physical location

Let's look more closely at both.

Online

There are many ways that people search for things online. It's important to be found in as many of these places that are relevant. Let's look at a couple examples:

- **Search engines.** A lot of people turn to Google, Bing, and Yahoo! when first looking for something online. Google, specifically, is often times the first place people turn when researching products, services, and causes, so it's very important to show up on the first page of Google's results for keywords that are important to you. You can do this by optimizing your website to appear organically at the top of the Google results page (this is referred to as "search engine optimization" or SEO). Or, you can pay per click to appear at the top of the results (this is referred to as "search engine marketing" or SEM).

  There are plenty of books and blogs written about each topic, so I won't get into more detail about SEO and SEM here. But if you're just getting started with a website, it is probably a good idea to invest in search engine marketing until your site can climb the ranks of the organic search engine results page. As a starting point, check out AdWords Express on Google. It makes search engine marketing easy and affordable.

- **Commerce sites like Amazon, Ebay, and the Apple App Store.** As the marketplace continues to grow online, some consumers are turning to sites like Amazon, Etsy, Ebay, and Zappos to look for product information. If you sell a product that is distributed via an online retailer, it's important to appear at the top of their search results page for keywords that matter to your organization.

  Similarly, if your business revolves around a mobile app, it's important to appear in the top results of relevant searches on Apple's App Store and Google Play. There are slight differences in the way in which you get to the top of the listings in each app store, so you should check out the store's best practice guides online for more information about each store.

Offline

To make sure passersby and people looking for you find you at your physical location, you should start by revisiting the items we discussed in the first part of this chapter: utilizing your physical assets. Being found in-person is all about your signage and other ways you are able to take advantage of your physical site. Use spotlights if you're hosting a grand opening. Or maybe get one of those big, inflatable animals to attract attention to your site if you're having a big sale or event.

More and more, though, consumers are turning to technology to find locations they are looking for. People are using websites like Google Maps, Bing Maps, and MapQuest on their mobile devices to find specific locations. You need to make sure that your offline location shows up properly online. As technology improves in ways that allow marketers to push messages to consumers on their phones when they pass by your location, people will become even more aware of your businesses if you take advantage of this emerging technology.

No matter where technology takes us, the bottom line is this: if someone is looking for your building, make sure they find it.

5. Offer an Engaging Way for Customers to Build a Community and Interact with Your Brand

In the Third Chapter of this book, we discussed how the best way to spread your messages quickly and efficiently is to give customers an experience worth sharing and then give them a way to share about it. That's what this must-have communication tool is all about. You need to provide customers or donors a way to interact with you and other customers about their experiences with your brand. This community could exist in one of many different formats:

- A Facebook fan page or group
- A weekly in-store club or regular gathering in which anybody can attend and participate
- A Twitter account
- A suggestion form on your website in which customers and donors weigh in on what they want to hear about from your organization, and you deliver that content regularly to their inbox via an e-newsletter
- A Pinterest board
- A YouTube channel
- The comments section of Yelp or another online distribution channel
- A blog or online message board

The important thing to remember about this tactic is that you only need to participate in one meaningful community to make this work. You don't need to maintain a community on every new online social media platform. You don't need to keep a blog, a Twitter account, send a weekly email, and post regularly to your YouTube channel. You just need to start by interacting with customers in one, engaging place. And you don't even have to create the community — you just need to participate in it in an honest, transparent way.

Coke has one of the most popular Facebook fan pages in the world, and it was actually created by two fans of the brand. For a while, marketers at Coke were happy to just participate in the dialogue happening on the page while the two fans maintained it. When Coke's Facebook page really took off and became extremely popular with millions of fans, the brand flew the page's two creators down to its headquarters in Atlanta and gave them the red carpet treatment. Coke gave the fans a tour of the World of Coke museum and a showed them the company's legendary archives. Coke marketing executives asked to gradually take over the Facebook page and the fans agreed to it. Coke did so in a respectful, transparent way that kept fans engaged with their content. The page is now a great vehicle for the brand to create a two-way dialogue with its customers.

If you are going to use an online social network to satisfy this marketing must-have, you need to monitor it regularly — at least once a week. You need to respond in a respectful, honest way to customer questions and complaints when they are posted to the social network. And you need to post a thank-you message when someone says something nice about you online. Above all else, treat your customers as you would like to be treated.

After the Five Must-Haves: Create a Customer Database

We spent a lot of the Second Chapter discussing how to segment target markets based on RFM+ models. Gathering customer data (with their permission) and using it to build effective marketing communication programs is very important. It's so important that I debated back and forth about including it as the sixth marketing communication must-have. However, I've come to the conclusion, based on my own experience and the many conversations I've had with startups, small businesses, and non-profits, that creating a customer database is not so important that you should stop everything you are doing in marketing communications in order to create one. That's the bar I've set for the five must-haves listed in this book. You should literally not do anything in marketing communications until you have put in place the five tactics outlined in this chapter. Building a customer database is important, but not *that* important.

If you're a startup and just getting started, you should take time to build a customer data collection system into your marketing communications plan before you go to market with your product or service. That's the best time to do it. When building your customer database, there are many data points you may wish to collect. In Chapter Two, I outlined some of those points. You will certainly want to capture other points than those, based on your specific needs as an organization. At a very basic level, you should capture these customer data points:

- Name
- Email address
- Phone number
- Physical address
- Date of birth
- Birth date
- Sex
- Purchase/donation dates
- Purchase/donation values

If you don't know how to start collecting customer data, consider putting into place these tactics that will generate customer data:

- An e-newsletter mailing list in which people submit information in order to read regular updates from you

- Website features behind a log-in screen; ask for a little bit of information from people and then provide them with enhanced content

- Online purchase data if you use a service like Paypal; if you sell things online, your payment solution provider will provide you with basic customer data for each purchase

- A "contact us for more information" form on your website

- Ask for basic information when someone calls your customer service phone line

- Customer relationship management software from a company like salesforce.com

Summary

There are five must-have marketing communication tactics that every startup, small business, and non-profit must undertake in order to ensure success. These are the building blocks on which all profitable marketing communication programs are built. Once these five tactics are in place, you can begin executing on the marketing communication tactics that you prioritized using Chapters Two through Five of this book.

chapter 7
IES Abroad redefines your world

It's time to bring everything together with an example that combines everything we've discussed in the first six chapters of this book. Before I arrived at Google, for more than five years I was fortunate to work for a small marketing department of five people at a great non-profit organization based in Chicago called IES Abroad — the Institute for the International Education of Students. IES Abroad provides study abroad programs for US college students. The organization functions very much like a US college with Deans, a Student Affairs department, a Registrar, Academic Advisors, and an Admissions department. Our Marketing department was in charge of all marketing communications. Our target markets included:

- Prospective students at our partner US colleges who were looking to study abroad — the goal was to convince them to apply to one of our study abroad programs

- Students who were admitted to our programs but hadn't enrolled or attended one yet — the goal was to convince them to attend our program instead of others to which they may have also applied

- Study abroad advisors within the study abroad offices at our US college partner institutions — the goal was to help the advisors understand the benefits of our programs so that they would recommend our programs to their students

- Alumni of our programs — the goal was to keep alumni engaged with our brand and donate to our scholarship fund

The Five Must-Haves

Let's first walk through the five must-have marketing communication tactics and look at how we implemented each of them at IES Abroad.

1. **Physical location** — while we had a nice corporate headquarters in Chicago, we very rarely had students or alumni into the office so it was not important for us to utilize our physical location in order to communicate with our target markets.

2. **Website** — we had a great website at www.IESabroad.org. On it, students could view the features of our different programs and apply directly to them.

3. **A way to speak to someone at the company** — outside of the marketing department, we had a team of 8-10 representatives that would interact with our partner school study abroad offices and potential students. We also had a nascent alumni relations team that would field calls from our alumni.

4. **Be found by our target markets** — IES Abroad invested in several forms of online advertising and search engine optimization to make sure that we were in the consideration set for prospective students looking to study abroad. We invested in Google AdWords to be found on Google, Facebook advertising solutions, and we bought online display ads on some of the most popular study abroad program aggregator's websites like studyabroad.com and goabroad.com.

5. **An engaging way to build a community and interact with our target markets** — we actually had several ways to do this. The three best were:

- **Facebook groups set up for each of our incoming groups of students, organized by the program in which they enrolled.** If you were a student who was admitted into a Spring program in Paris, you would be invited to join a Facebook group with fellow Spring Paris program students before your program began. In that group, an IES Abroad Advisor would interact with students who had questions before studying abroad, but the group was mostly intended for students to get to know each other before meeting abroad.

- **Student bloggers.** Each term, IES Abroad featured 30 student bloggers on its blog site. These bloggers were chosen to write about their experiences abroad via an application process. The bloggers committed to posting updates at least three times per month while studying abroad. Prospective students, study abroad advisors, alumni, and the bloggers' families would often interact with the bloggers via comments on the blogging platform.

- **A quarterly magazine sent to all alumni and friends of IES Abroad.** This magazine would update everybody on what was going on at the organization and with their former classmates. The publication was just like an alumni magazine from a college. It featured alumni notes from former students about where they were living and what they had been up to since studying abroad.

A Brand [Redefined]

In my last year at IES Abroad, our small but mighty marketing team set out on a re-branding mission. We needed to consolidate our branding messages into one cohesive message that we could use in all of our marketing communications to all of our target markets. We needed one simple, powerful, shareable message that would resonate with our target markets. We were also trying to increase the pool of students around the country who were interested in studying abroad. Our goal was to both increase the number of students interested in studying abroad and increase the number of students studying with IES Abroad. It was a big undertaking, but we were up to the challenge.

One day, we hunkered down in a conference room for an all-day brainstorming session about the re-brand. Now, the company conference room isn't exactly the greatest place to draw inspiration for big ideas, but it actually worked. By the end of the day, we had identified the unique proposition of studying abroad and had thought of some great ways of activating our message. Our main idea centered on a very simple phrase:

your world [redefined]

All of our target markets could engage with that message. For prospective students, the message was that studying abroad would redefine their world. For alumni, the message was meant to remind them of how much their world had been redefined by their study abroad experience.

To bring this message to life with a very limited budget, we knew we had to create a marketing communication plan that would really inspire our target markets to share the message with their peers. We knew we had to invest our time and limited money in marketing communication tactics that inspired sharing and were easy to share. We first decided to put our message in the hands of our current students and encourage them to share with their friends and families how their worlds had been redefined.

We created simple signs printed on standard white pieces paper that said, "_____ [redefined]" and we sent them to students around the world, invited them to write in the blank space something in their world that had been redefined because of studying abroad, and then share what they wrote via pictures and videos. We were blown away at the response — both how quickly it gained traction among students and how creative our students became in what they wrote.

In short order, students started participating and sharing photos and videos on their favorite social media channels. Some of the photos showed:

- Students at European and South American soccer games holding signs saying "football [redefined]"

- Students on camels in Morocco holding signs saying, "morning commute [redefined]"

- Students learning to make crème brûlée in Paris, holding blowtorches and signs saying, "playing with fire [redefined]"

- Students standing in front of remnants of the Berlin wall holding signs saying, "freedom [redefined]"

- Students walking through the outback in Australia holding signs saying, "the walk to class [redefined]"

- Students at the top of the Machu Picchu overlook in Peru holding signs saying, "getting high [redefined]"

The opportunities for creativity were infinite. We knew we were onto something when in just the first few weeks of rolling out the campaign, students emailed us dozens of photos. They also began posting them on their own Facebook pages and sharing them with their friends. As more and more students began sharing how studying abroad had redefined them, we saw that they were reaching our most important target market — current college students at our partner universities. And they were doing so in an engaging, honest way.

This wasn't a gimmick. It was a genuine expression of the impact of studying abroad.

This marketing tactic scored highly on both sets of criteria outlined in the Third Chapter of this book: we provided experiences worth sharing and then made it extremely easy for those experiences to be shared. Thousands of students ended up sharing our message with their friends and family at nearly no cost to us. It was remarkable.

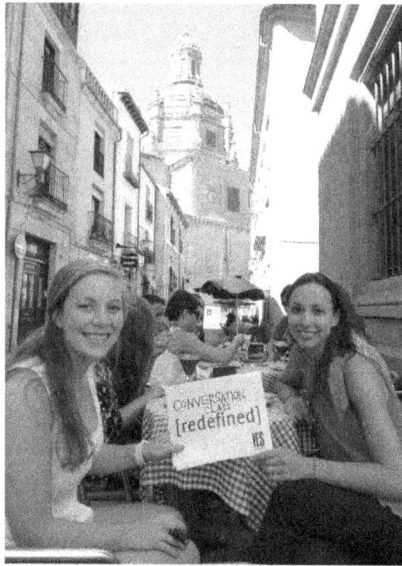

Students studying with IES Abroad in Salamanca, Spain show their redefined conversation class. Photo courtesy of IES Abroad.

Alumni [Redefined]

Soon after our students began posting pictures online of themselves holding their redefined signs, we began seeing our alumni getting in on the act, too. IES Abroad alumni working in great jobs around the world began posting their own signs about how studying abroad had redefined their world and impacted their career choice. We envisioned all kinds of possibilities:

- A teacher in a developing country holding a sign saying, "9-5 job [redefined]"

- Alumni at a program reunion holding signs saying, "social networking [redefined]"

- A volunteer near a well in a rural community holding a sign saying "chatting around the water cooler [redefined]"

Integrating the Concept into Every Marketing Tactic

The entire [redefined] campaign involved many marketing communication tactics. If we were to plot them on prioritization charts, all of the tactics we executed would fall in the first quadrant. They reached our target market and they were worth sharing and easy to share.

- All of our printed materials that we sent to students and study abroad offices featured pictures of students holding [redefined] signs. This included giant posters for our partners in study abroad offices and all kinds of printed catalogs, brochures, and fliers

- We revamped our website to incorporate [redefined] images and language

- We created a Facebook photo gallery of students holding their [redefined] signs and encouraged students to tag themselves and share them with their friends

- On our Twitter account, we posted links to the photos on our Facebook gallery frequently

- We created short videos of students holding their [redefined] signs and posted them to our YouTube channel on a regular basis

Return on Marketing Investment

At this point, you're probably wondering how we measured the return on our marketing investment for this campaign. We were able to measure many of our online tactics through Google Analytics and offline tactics via manual data collection. For example, when a new student lead came to us online, we used our online registration form to ask her how she heard about us. If she came to us via an in-person meeting with one of our representatives, our representative simply asked her how she heard about us. These collection methods enabled us to record which marketing communication tactic was responsible for every lead.

When I left IES Abroad, we were just beginning conversations around creating one all-inclusive dashboard on which we could evaluate the return on our marketing investments across all communication channels.

Accolades

The IES Abroad [redefined] campaign was extremely well received by our students, alumni, study abroad advisor partners, and the entire study abroad industry. The campaign won an incredible number of marketing awards, including top honors from the Higher Education Advertising Awards, the Service Industry Advertising Awards, the Council for Advancement and Support of Education, the Trumpet Awards, the GoAbroad.com Innovation Awards, the Communicator Awards, and the Business Marketing Association.

The campaign was the most decorated in the history of the study abroad industry, and it continues to live on today. IES Abroad continues to be innovative in its use of the [redefined] theme, and students continue to enjoy sharing their study abroad experiences with their friends, families, and potential new students in this way.

chapter 8
get your priorities straight

We've come to the end of the book, and it's time for you to put everything we've discussed into action. What follows are some questions designed to get you to reflect back on each section of this book and help you get started on setting marketing communication priorities:

1. Are you reaching your target markets?

- Do you know who your target markets are? Who are your best customers? How can you engage with more people like them?

- Have you identified your searchers? How do people search for you or your products, services, or cause?

- Are there groups of people who are passionate about something for which your offerings align? How can you reach these passion markets?

- Are there events in people's lives that will trigger them into being in the market for your product or service? How can you reach these trigger markets?

- If you are collecting customer data, are you able to create a customer segmentation model based on recency, frequency, and monetary value? How can you drive more revenue based on those customer segments?

- What other pieces of customer data matter to your business or non-profit? And how can you turn that information into a customer segmentation strategy that will allow you to better customize your marketing communications?

- Are you prioritizing your marketing communication tactics based on reaching your target markets?

2. **Are your marketing communications creating experiences worth sharing that are easy to share?**

   - Are you educating, inspiring, or entertaining your target markets with your marketing communications or are you just shouting promotional messages at them? Think back to the Honor Flight. Are you giving people an unforgettable experience that makes an impact on their lives?

   - Are you inviting people to share with their friends the experiences they have with your brand? Think about the signs sent from IES Abroad to current students abroad.

   - Are you making it easy for people to share their experiences with your brand? Are you putting your content online so it can be shared with an email, tweet, or a "like"?

   - Are you prioritizing marketing communication tactics that are worth sharing and easy to share?

3. **Are you prioritizing your marketing communication tactics based on return on marketing investment?**

   - Have you put into place a way to track success metrics for your marketing communication tactics?

   - Are you assigning values to your marketing communications based on direct and indirect financial outcomes?

- Are you working toward building a complete understanding about the financial impact of all your marketing communication tactics?

- Are you prioritizing marketing communications based on how each tactic contributes to your bottom line?

4. **Do you have the five must-have marketing communication tactics in place?**

   - If you have a brick-and-mortar presence, have you taken advantage of the marketing communication opportunities your location provides? Do you have a sign out front featuring your name and what you do?

   - Do you have a website? Are you updating it at least once per month?

   - Are you providing your customers and potential customers with a way to speak to someone at your company?

   - Can your target markets find you? Do you show up near the top of search engine results pages for relevant searches? If someone is looking for your organization, will they find it easily?

   - Are you engaging your target market in at least one community in which customers can interact with you and their like-minded peers?

An Invitation to Share This Book with Your Friends

Now it's my turn: I humbly ask you to share this book with your friends if you found it helpful. Feel free to write an honest review of what you thought of this book in the place in which you acquired it. If you downloaded the PDF, please write a review on Amazon. If you feel inclined to share about this book via social networks, remember to use #marketingpriorities. I'm trying to start a movement with that hashtag. Join me!

I also invite you to let me know what you thought of the ideas I've presented here. Where was I wrong? Where was I right? Do you have your own examples of how you have prioritized your marketing communications? I'd love to hear directly from you. Look me up online at **www.nickscarpino.com** and send me a message.

I wish you and your business or non-profit all the best. Thanks for reading.

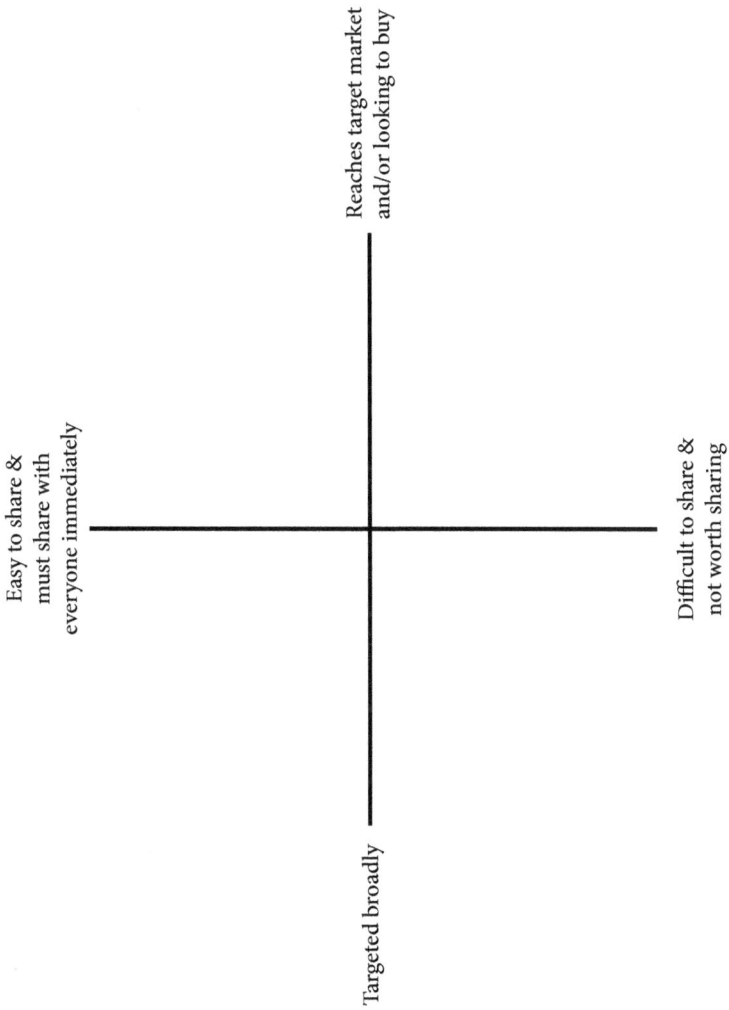

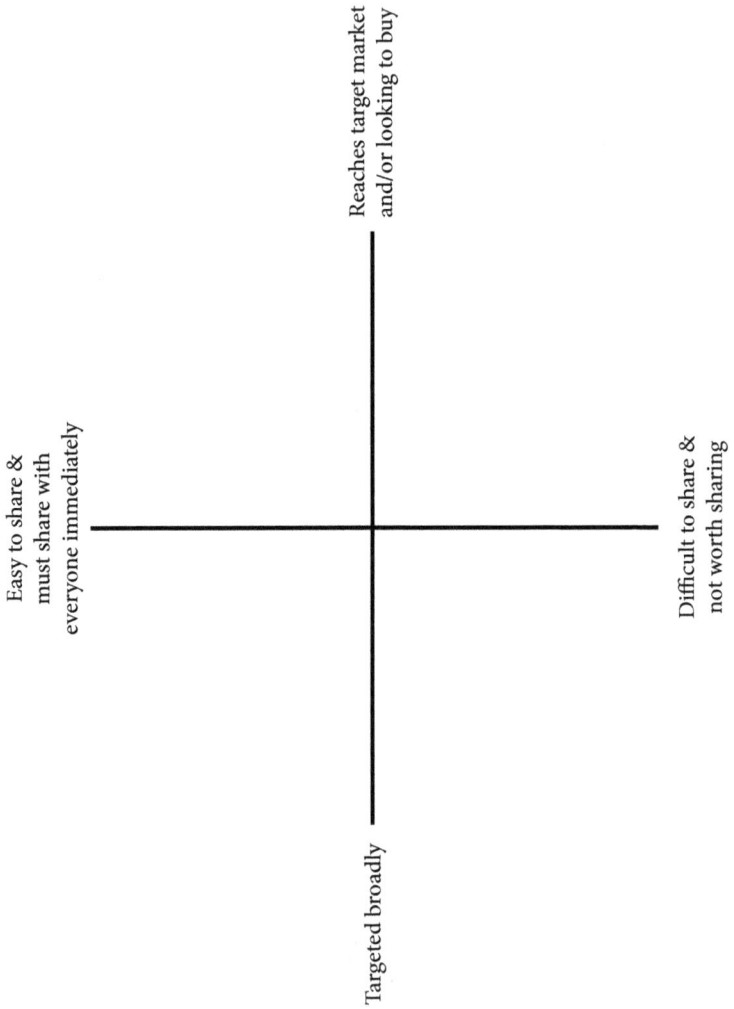

thank you
acknowledgements

There are a lot of people who helped make this book possible. I am forever grateful for all who gave me insightful feedback and encouraged me to see it all the way through. A sincere thank you to:

- My immediate and extended family for their love and support.

- Bill Shields for convincing me that my original title and introduction left a lot to be desired.

- Amy McMillan for never letting me sell myself short.

- Courtney Peters for knowing the *Chicago Manual of Style* like the back of her hand.

- My Google coworkers for their thoughtful input and advice: Jackie Loo, Kellen Meranus, Katy Galambos, Blake Twisselman, Matt Jones, Megan Danielson, and Jim Lecinski.

- Avinash Kaushik for graciously writing the foreword.

- Everyone who has ever read my blog, *Never a Lack of Ideas,* and commented on a post or shared it with a friend.

www.ingramcontent.com/pod-product-compliance
Lightning Source LLC
Chambersburg PA
CBHW060627210326
41520CB00010B/1496